ULTIMATE
OUTDOOR KITCHENS

ULTIMATE
OUTDOOR KITCHENS

Inspirational Designs and Plans

MICHELLE KODIS

Gibbs Smith, Publisher
SALT LAKE CITY

First Edition
10 09 08 07 06   5 4 3 2 1

Published by
Gibbs Smith, Publisher
P.O. Box 667
Layton, Utah 84041

Orders: 1.800.748.5439
www.gibbs-smith.com

Designed by Gretchen Scoble
Printed and bound in Hong Kong

Library of Congress Cataloging-in-Publication Data

Kodis, Michelle.
  Ultimate outdoor kitchens : inspirational designs and plans / Michelle
Kodis.—1st ed.
     p. cm.
  ISBN 1-58685-791-6
  1. Outdoor living spaces. 2. Kitchens. 3. Landscape architecture.
I. Title.

NK2117.O87K64 2006
747'.8893—dc22

2006010742

For Rich, a genius at the grill and the love of my life.

CONTENTS

ACKNOWLEDGMENTS

Hearty thanks and appreciation to: Gibbs Smith, Suzanne Taylor, Christopher Robbins, Hollie Keith, Kurt Wahlner, Alison Einerson, Laura Ayrey, Carrie Westover and Anita Wood, the wonderful people at Gibbs Smith, Publisher; the designers and photographers whose projects and images helped to shape this book; my husband, Rich; the Kodis and Cieciuch families; Andrew and Brett; my fabulous friends; Violet, who gets me outside every day; and Roscoe, for the countless memories. Special thanks to Maureen, who rushed in to rescue me just when I needed it, and Rosemerry, who wrote the perfect poem on such short notice.

INTRODUCTION

The rising popularity of outdoor living, which is about finding new ways to connect our homes to their environments, has paved the way for the outdoor kitchen—and we're not talking about a freestanding grill on the patio (which does have its merit). Today's outdoor kitchen runs the gamut from a simple cook station to a fully appointed outdoor room, but regardless of the design or the budget, the goal is the same: cook outside, eat outside—in short, find any excuse to be outside. But in truth, this book is about much more than kitchens: it's an exploration of how we can combine, through cutting-edge architecture and design, the two fundamental human needs for food and fresh air.

When you think about it, the modern outdoor kitchen really is nothing more than a sophisticated extension of the campfire. People have been preparing their food alfresco for millennia. Who doesn't have a memory of a campfire and the pleasure of watching the flames stretch toward the sky? (Although I can remember a particularly exuberant campfire at my brother-in-law's mountain cabin, where the s'mores were being cranked out as though on a production line, that ended up setting the yard on fire—but that's an entirely different story, and one that fortunately had a happy ending.)

My own memories of campfires and cooking outdoors can be recalled easily. As a child, I spent a week at an Outward Bound program in Wales. We moved through the backcountry like intrepid explorers, not afraid to get wet or lost, and we practiced cooking our (very basic) food over fire. On a snow camping trip in the mountains of south-western Colorado, I learned the joy of instant oatmeal prepared over a gas flame. Float trips down Utah's San Juan River brought me the pure, childlike joy of making lasagna in a cast-iron Dutch oven—what a miracle that was, and it tasted good, too. Trekking through Nepal, I bunked in "tea houses" along the trail and would wake each morning to the aroma of breakfast being prepared at the host's always-stoked fireplace. These days, my husband (aka grill master, as we call him, not to be confused with the manufacturer) whips up grilled salmon that's so good I refuse to order it in most restaurants because I suspect it won't match his recipe and method of preparation. I could go on, but you get the picture.

When I was asked to write this book, at first I wasn't sure how to proceed. Would I pen a technical manual for do-it-yourselfers, and include detailed accounts of how to build an outdoor kitchen on the weekend? What kinds of kitchens would I feature? Most importantly, how could I best present the material to a wide scope of readers, all presumed to have different budgets, design preferences and lifestyles?

The answers arrived as the projects began to pour into my office. I culled them until I had twenty-six kitchens with the greatest diversity in terms of style and functionality, as well as broad geographic range. Then I decided to organize the kitchens into sections filled with separate chapters illustrated with color photographs, for clear and easy navigation on the part of the reader. Those sections evolved into *Just the Basics, Creative Functionality* and *Going All Out*. In *Just the Basics,* you will find exactly that: simple, budget-friendly cooking stations with plenty of character and individuality. In *Creative Functionality,* the outdoor kitchen starts to get a little more snazzy, with additional appliances and special design elements and materials. And in *Going All Out,* you'll read about outdoor kitchens equipped with lots of bells and whistles and in many cases designed without strict budgetary limitations. Throughout the text you'll also find short tips to help you on your way to creating a great outdoor kitchen.

As you read, keep in mind that an outdoor kitchen is not just about materials, design and position in the yard; its purpose extends to the experience of being outside. As we increasingly strive to connect our homes to their environments, whether urban, suburban or rural, we can discover many opportunities to interact with nature, even if "nature" is a backyard just steps from a neighboring house.

Your outdoor kitchen can be as simple or as elaborate as you desire and your budget allows—but again, that's not the entire point of this book. As you read, try to call up your own memories of being outside with a cooked meal before you on the table or balanced on a paper plate on your lap or eaten straight out of the pot. What is it that makes a meal cooked outside taste so wonderful? Of course, that's part of the mystery. For now, we move on to practicalities: kitchen designs, materials, ways to build and which appliances to choose. The memories—well, those will becomes yours, and yours alone.

Bon appétit!

—Michelle Kodis

How to Redeem the Distractible Chef

By Rosemerry Wahtola Trommer

Evening, and the wild orange sun
still warmed the patio boards.
Stellar's jays squawked in the yard,
and the lancet cottonwood leaves
had just begun to turn.
So perfect, the landscape,
I let the grilled eggplant burn.
I knew it was almost done, of course,
had tenderly flipped the purple-skinned discs
just as the centers had started to pooch,
and poof!
I was held with the way the wind
tickles the tips of tall grass in the field
and the sound of white laughter
as the river fidgets against its stone bed.
I should have been tending my eggplant,
marinated with garlic, fresh basil and oil.
Instead, I was rapt with the sun on my back
and the whirr of the rose-throated hummingbirds,
and the sweet green smell of fresh cut grass.
Within minutes, the eggplant had charred to black.
And so with a sigh I placed it on plates
beside linguine al dente
and thick slabs of vine-ripened tomato.
And we ate as the sun relaxed in the west,
joined by jays, hummingbirds, and of course the flies.
It was a burned meal, yes, but amazingly good—
everything tastes better when you eat it outside.

JUST THE BASICS

Artistic Backyard Barbecue Station

DESIGN: Scott Cohen, The Green Scene
PHOTOGRAPHS: Deidra Walpole

LOCATION: *Santa Barbara, California*
FEATURES: *gas grill with rotisserie, under-counter refrigerator, stain-resistant counter*
KEY MATERIALS: *concrete, river stone, Arizona flagstone*
SPECIAL TOUCHES: *custom ceramic tile accents, wood pergola, water features, firepit*

This simple outdoor kitchen reveals how a few out-of-the-ordinary design elements can elevate even the most basic barbecue station into an artistic statement.

Designed by landscape specialist Scott Cohen, the stand-alone unit is one component of a multifunctional backyard that includes a covered dining/seating patio, a man-made waterfall and stream, a spa and a firepit. Despite the size constraints of the small yard, Cohen effectively united each individual element in an arrangement of space that looks and feels like an outdoor room.

By placing the barbecue just beyond the indoor kitchen, Cohen was able to keep it streamlined without sacrificing functionality: foods can be stored and prepped indoors and then transported outside for cooking. The barbecue unit, a cinder block form clad in flagstone veneer and accented with river rock, houses a stainless steel gas grill/rotisserie combination, a refrigerator and storage drawers. A cast concrete counter is an excellent choice for outdoor kitchens thanks to its weather- and stain-resistant properties and the fact that it won't collect food particles as a counter with grout can do if not sealed properly. Custom ceramic tiles in a variety of leaf shapes adorn the station's arched backsplash, adding color, texture and subtle ornamentation.

The dining/seating patio highlights the beauty of Arizona flagstone pavers and is protected by a Douglas fir pergola painted to match the house. Because the house backs up to a road, finding a way to reduce traffic noise was crucial; Cohen responded to this challenge by installing water features that bring a peaceful atmosphere to the yard.

KITCHENS 101

Before you begin, become knowledgeable about your local building and fire safety codes, and be aware of any restrictions regarding the size and location of the kitchen.

A painted Douglas fir pergola helps shade the dining/seating patio, covered in Arizona flagstone pavers in a four-color combination. The designer installed water features, including a stream and waterfall, to help block traffic noise from a nearby road. The stream separates the patio and firepit seating area.

FACING: The barbecue station—located just beyond the interior kitchen and outfitted with a grill, under-counter refrigerator and storage drawers—has a streamlined design that doesn't impact functionality. The proximity of the indoor and outdoor kitchens makes it convenient to prep foods inside and then bring them outside for cooking.

ABOVE RIGHT: The stainless steel gas grill/rotisserie sits securely in a cinder block box covered with flagstone veneer and river rock accents. The counter is smooth cast concrete, a good choice for an outdoor kitchen because it is weather- and stain-resistant and won't trap food particles as grout can sometimes do.

BELOW RIGHT: Custom ceramic tiles in the shapes of leaves by artist Michelle Griffoul and a light fixture by Bruce Dennis add color and texture to the backsplash, formed with stucco-clad bullnose block.

Rustic Southwestern Style

DESIGN: Catherine Clemens, Clemens & Associates

PHOTOGRAPHS: Catherine Clemens and Robert Reck

LOCATION: *Santa Fe, New Mexico*

FEATURES: *built-in gas grill with side burner, under-counter refrigerator*

KEY MATERIALS: *stucco, limestone, redwood*

SPECIAL TOUCHES: *raised planter filled with culinary herbs, adjacent negative-edge pool/spa*

Landscape architect Catherine Clemens gave this modest but stylish outdoor kitchen two important attributes: beautiful materials and low-maintenance functionality.

Located in the backyard of a house blessed with sweeping west-facing views of Santa Fe, New Mexico, the kitchen shares space with a negative-edge pool/spa and dining patio. Positioned close to the interior dining and entertainment areas for indoor/outdoor access, the kitchen is partially enclosed by stucco walls that help separate it from the rest of the space but allow the cook to move easily between the cooking area and patio. Working with just a few materials—stucco, limestone and redwood—Clemens designed a kitchen with a straightforward look and plenty of practicality. The gas grill is built into a stucco-clad concrete block island accented with redwood cabinet doors. A long prep counter, side burner, under-counter refrigerator, sink, electrical outlets and a nearby raised planter filled with culinary herbs provide the cook with just the right tools for creating a great meal. As cold weather approaches, the kitchen can be winterized simply by shutting off the water and draining the sink. A canvas cover can be used to protect the grill.

Due to high-altitude Santa Fe's short growing season, Clemens opted to make the hardscape the focus of the yard. "Instead of taking a plant-based approach, we introduced strong lines and interesting materials," she says. "By not making the plants the main feature, the clients have an outdoor room that looks good year-round."

WATER WISDOM

If you want an outdoor sink, be prepared to spend extra money to extend water and waste lines from the house. If the outdoor kitchen is positioned near the indoor kitchen, a sink or other appliance requiring plumbing might not be necessary. An alternative to a fully plumbed sink is a portable unit hooked to a garden hose.

Large sandstone boulders at the edge of the pool separate it from the kitchen enclosure, one side of which features a raised planter containing a variety of culinary herbs. *Photo by Catherine Clemens.*

ABOVE: The kitchen's honed limestone counter and backsplash complement the French limestone patio. Ample below-counter storage keeps utensils and cookware close at hand, and the cook can quickly clip herbs from the adjacent planter. To winterize the kitchen, the owners only have to shut off the water, drain the sink and cover the grill. Durable redwood was chosen for the cabinets and will hold up to Santa Fe's cold, snowy winters. The redwood adds color to the toned-down styling of the stucco kitchen enclosure. *Photo by Catherine Clemens.*

FACING: Thanks to a landscape design that emphasizes hardscape features rather than plants, the yard retains its beauty year-round in Santa Fe's relatively short growing season. The patio gives way to a curved negative-edge pool/spa.
Photo by Robert Reck.

The revamped backyard is now more spacious and inviting, with separate zones joined by flagstone walkways and defined by the use of materials. The owners wanted a low-maintenance yard, accomplished here with tidy arrangements of plants interspersed with hardscape features.

Budget-Conscious Outdoor Kitchen

DESIGN: Michelle Van de Voorde, Elemental Design Group

PHOTOGRAPHS: Gregory Case

LOCATION: *Saratoga, California*
FEATURES: *built-in gas grill accented by colorful stone work, large dining patio*
KEY MATERIALS: *bluestone, brick, flagstone, honed slate*
SPECIAL TOUCHES: *gas firepit, fountain*

Simplicity is translated into elegance and beauty in this remodeled suburban backyard. Designed by landscape architect Michelle Van de Voorde, the space went from ordinary—a bulky wood deck attached to the house, a patch of lawn and some perimeter plantings—to visually engaging and more inviting.

Van de Voorde's clients put about $100,000 into their new backyard, a budget that dictated a pared-down outdoor kitchen with just a built-in gas grill—a functional but affordable option. To create the look and feel of an outdoor room, they also invested in a spacious dining patio, fountain, gas firepit and hot tub set into a platform several steps above the garden. A stone seating wall flanks the cooking station—a recommended feature for any outdoor space where large gatherings are expected to take place. New French doors lead from the master bedroom straight out to the yard, now organized into "areas of distinction in what used to be an uninteresting space," the architect explains.

"Instead of stacking the hardscape features up against the back of the house, we instead created a destination out in the garden," she adds. "The result is a series of zones that dance together, creating flow and movement in the yard versus the static feeling that had been there before. Now there is the sense of wanting to move through the yard."

Also important to the owners was minimal upkeep, accomplished here with low-maintenance plants in tidy arrangements that stay beautiful year-round, and stone and concrete patios and walkways that only need to be swept now and then. The barbecue unit is just as easy to maintain thanks to stain-resistant sealed slate counters. Even with a limited selection of materials—primarily flagstone, Chief Cliff fieldstone, bluestone, brick and concrete—Van de Voorde brought artistic flair to the yard by juxtaposing the materials to take best advantage of their colors and textures.

GOING PREFAB

If you can't afford a custom outdoor kitchen or don't have the time or desire to build one or work with a designer, a prefab grill island could be an option. Prices begin at about $1,000 for a basic grill counter setup and go to $30,000 or more for kitchen/bar/entertainment units that can include everything from a cooking center to a flat-screen television with DVD player.

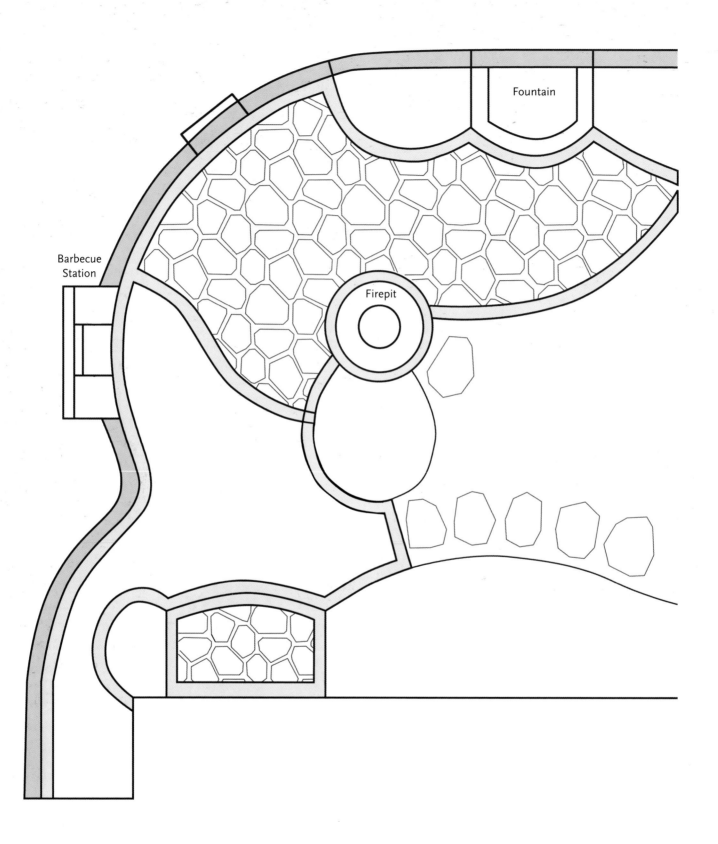

Fountain

Barbecue
Station

Firepit

Materials, including bluestone slate pavers and brick, were chosen to complement the traditional ranch-style architecture of the house. The patio easily accommodates an outdoor dining table, gas firepit and fountain. The firepit is filled with lava rock and capped with bluestone.

ABOVE: Interlocking concrete pavers visually separate the barbecue from the dining patio. Less expensive than stone, the pavers helped keep the budget in check.

FACING: The cooking station is conveniently positioned next to the dining patio. The gas grill is set into a concrete block unit clad in Chief Cliff stone veneer and topped with a honed slate counter. The seating wall is Chief Cliff fieldstone with a bluestone cap.

Sheltered Patio Kitchen

DESIGN: Katheryn Lott

PHOTOGRAPHS: Greg Hursley

LOCATION: *Austin, Texas*

FEATURES: *gas grill cooking station just steps from the indoor kitchen*

KEY MATERIALS: *Texas sandstone and lueders limestone*

SPECIAL TOUCHES: *ceiling fan to help circulate breezes through the covered dining patio, long-lasting teak furniture*

In some parts of the country, an agreeable climate makes an outdoor kitchen an easy choice. This Austin home had another thing going for it: a beautiful treed site that motivated architect Katheryn Lott to give her clients year-round indoor/outdoor dining and entertainment options.

By emphasizing natural materials, primarily stone and wood, Lott designed a home that nestles discreetly into its setting. As she studied the site, she paid close attention to sun angle and wind patterns, factors that prompted her decision to place a covered porch along the east side of the building, where prevailing southeastern breezes cool the space (a western orientation would have been too sunny and hot). Proximity to the interior kitchen made the porch the perfect place for outdoor cooking and dining, and Lott was careful to ensure easy access between indoors and out via tall glass doors.

Located just steps from the indoor kitchen, the outdoor kitchen is straightforward but functional: a stainless steel gas grill with storage below, and a few electrical outlets. Lott added character and enhanced the continuity of the overall design theme by placing the grill into a sandstone surround and using lueders limestone for the counter—materials also found elsewhere on the house. Arches positioned along the porch act as windows, framing the thick stands of cedar trees that Lott was adamant about preserving during construction.

A small courtyard leads to the front entrance of the home. The architecture reflects a Mediterranean influence, characterized by deep overhangs for sun protection and clay tiles.

The cook enjoys expansive views of the treed setting.

LEFT: The orientation of the L-shaped porch protects it from too much sun exposure and captures the prevailing southeastern breezes to cool the space. Texas sandstone was used on the exterior of the house, as well as indoors. The railing is painted wrought iron.

FACING: Mediterranean-style arches soften the lines of the porch and frame views of the mature cedar trees surrounding the house. Raising the porch a few feet off the ground enhanced the private feel of the space. The primary materials on the porch are Texas sandstone (walls and arches), lueders limestone (patio pavers and kitchen counter) and stained Douglas fir (ceiling).

FACING: The stainless steel gas grill is set into a base constructed of Texas sandstone and topped with a sealed lueders limestone counter. A storage niche below holds cooking utensils.

RIGHT: The interior kitchen is just steps from the outdoor kitchen, for quick access and a convenient indoor/outdoor connection.

Built for the Elements

DESIGN: Cameron Nagel and Rob Robinson

PHOTOGRAPHS: Cameron Nagel

LOCATION: *Neskowin, Oregon*

FEATURES: *sturdy wood-fired barbecue with separate oven*

KEY MATERIALS: *stone and firebrick*

SPECIAL TOUCHES: *low chimney that allows smoke to envelop the grill, imparting flavor to food*

Cameron Nagel, a self-described "foodie" and the editor and publisher of *Northwest Palate Magazine,* is always on the lookout for new ways to cook and present food. And, as a former building contractor, he also knows his way around a set of plans. Those skills went hand in hand when he decided to add a custom outdoor kitchen to the patio of his weekend house in the quaint village of Neskowin, located on the Oregon Coast.

The home's spacious patio allowed Nagel and his codesigner, stonemason Rob Robinson, to think big. The result is a substantial wood-fired barbecue and oven that together create a versatile cooking environment: for example, Nagel can bake a pizza and barbecue a chicken at the same time. Along with versatility, Nagel wanted a welcoming setting that would encourage guests to cozy up to the fire while the food is being prepped and cooked. With its wide stone counters and ample length, the cooking station invites people to mill about while the food is being prepared and, once the food is done, to stand at the counter and nibble.

The cooking station is conveniently positioned just off the main kitchen, where double doors provide a direct indoor/ outdoor connection and the ability to quickly transfer food from inside to out or vice versa. The waist-high grill and work surfaces make standing and grilling a comfortable task, and separate flues for the grill and oven give the cook greater control of each heat source. Nagel and Robinson kept the chimney relatively short, a design technique that allows wood smoke to engulf the food—and more smoke means more flavor.

Yet another factor to consider was the coastal climate, which frequently brings strong winds and plenty of rain. Heavy-duty stone elements anchor the cooking station firmly to the ground—this outdoor kitchen is in no danger of blowing away in the wind. And, because the station has no mechanical parts, maintenance is minimal: Nagel only has to clean out the ashes now and then, which in turn gives him more time to dream up new recipes.

For Nagel, the opportunity to cook over wood was irresistible. Content enough with the gas grill at his primary residence in urban Portland, the lure of smoke-infused, exotically flavored foods called to him when he began to design his weekend outdoor kitchen. "Being a city dweller who uses charcoal or gas on a regular basis, I was ready to begin experimenting with foods cooked on real wood," he says. "Wood imparts simple and honest flavors to food."

Located just off the main kitchen, the combination
wood-fired barbecue and oven cooking station is
versatile and tailored to informal gatherings. The
barbecue and oven vent through separate flues for
greater heat control, and the short chimney forces
smoke onto the food, infusing it with subtle flavors
and scents from the wood. The arch over the barbecue is lined with firebrick. Here, the designer's friends
enjoy a casual cookout.

LEFT: Built to withstand the coastal climate, the cooking station has a cinder block core and is covered with Montana Mossy ledge stone, each piece hand cut, chiseled and fit together. Wide counters provide plenty of room for setting out platters of food.

FACING ABOVE: The oven's bronze doors reflect the stone used on the cooking station, and recessed mortar joints add to the rustic nature of the design.

FACING BELOW: Iron Mountain flagstone, chosen for its variegated color, was used for the flat surfaces and also on the patio.

FACING RIGHT: When engulfed by smoke, food takes on the flavor of the wood being used. The designer, also an avid cook, prefers cherry, maple and oak for their flavors and because they efficiently build and maintain heat in the coals.

Contemporary Open-Air Kitchen

DESIGN: Colleen Holmes, New Leaf Landscape

PHOTOGRAPHS: Deidra Walpole

LOCATION: *Beverly Hills, California*
FEATURES: *separate grill island and food prep/dining counters*
KEY MATERIALS: *granite, limestone*
SPECIAL TOUCHES: *koi pond, waterfall*

This contemporary California home had all the makings of a great outdoor living space complete with open-air kitchen and dining patio, but an unattractive concrete patio and a pond in desperate need of a redo kept it from realizing its true potential.

Landscape designer Colleen Holmes saw the possibilities in the property immediately, despite the challenges of the site—in particular, the seen-better-days concrete and pond, and a hillside location that made adding retaining walls and other hardscape features a complex prospect.

Perhaps the most compelling argument for an outdoor room with a kitchen/dining area was the home's floor plan: all of its rooms open to a private courtyard in a configuration that all but demanded a more direct indoor/outdoor connection. Judging from the property's new appearance, Holmes has successfully transformed the yard into an elegant, welcoming space. The concrete has been replaced with a creamy limestone that brightens the courtyard and is kind to bare feet, and the pond was cleaned out and given fresh materials. The outdoor spaces are split on two levels—kitchen, dining patio, fireplace and pond on the lower level, and pool on the upper level. Lush plantings bring a touch of bold color to the monochromatic palette.

Holmes placed the outdoor kitchen right off the indoor kitchen and separated the grill island and food prep/dining counters to maximize the square footage of the space. The kitchen includes a gas grill, under-counter refrigerator and below-counter storage.

HOW HIGH?

How high should your counters be? A comfortable standing height for working the grill is thirty-six inches, and bar-height seating should be at forty-two to forty-six inches.

The rooms of the house open to a private courtyard, for an effortless indoor/outdoor connection. The old concrete patio was replaced with smooth limestone, which imparts a clean look and is comfortable to walk on barefoot. Lush landscaping brings warmth and color to the contemporary styling of the house and yard.

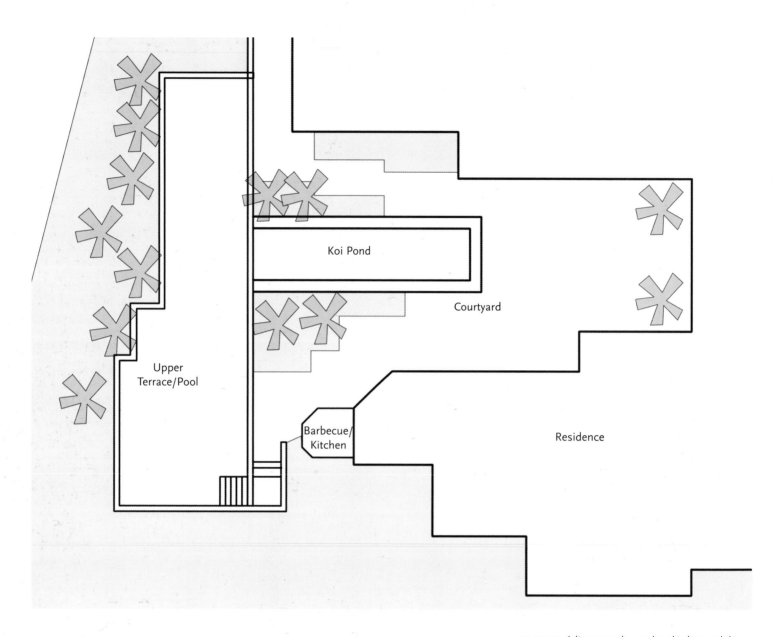

Koi Pond

Courtyard

Upper
Terrace/Pool

Barbecue/
Kitchen

Residence

ABOVE: The outdoor kitchen is located off the interior kitchen for quick transport of food and cookware. The upper terrace houses a pool and is connected to the kitchen level by a stair.

FACING: Separating the grill island and food prep/ bar counter gave the outdoor kitchen plenty of room and guarded against potential physical obstructions between it and the rest of the patio. The counters are granite with a flamed finish.

Santa Fe Kitchen Enclosure

DESIGN: Catherine Clemens, Clemens & Associates

PHOTOGRAPHS: Catherine Clemens

LOCATION: *Santa Fe, New Mexico*
FEATURES: *separate kitchen enclosure stepped down from main patio*
KEY MATERIALS: *Arizona flagstone, sandstone, stucco, granite*
SPECIAL TOUCHES: *salvaged mesquite gate cut and crafted into cabinet doors*

An old mesquite gate found new life in this outdoor kitchen located north of Santa Fe, New Mexico, within earshot of the famed Santa Fe Opera.

Designed by landscape architect Catherine Clemens, the kitchen's earthy materials and adobe-style enclosure give it a rustic appearance that plays off the style of the house, which Clemens describes as "contemporary with a hint of primitive elements." Such primitive elements in the kitchen include the above-mentioned mesquite gate, which was cut into pieces for cabinet doors. The mesquite is weather-resistant and requires only periodic oiling to retain its rich color.

The positioning of the outdoor kitchen was influenced by the two-level design of the yard: the kitchen is on the upper level and a pool is on the lower level. In order to make the kitchen a true destination within the yard, Clemens surrounded it with low adobe-style walls and recessed it several steps below the patio. Although the enclosure walls resemble traditional adobe, in reality they are a decidedly modern interpretation: concrete block covered in stucco. Granite-capped perimeter benches provide seating for those who wish to keep the cook company.

Because the site spans several acres and has views that seem to go on forever, Clemens worked her landscape plan around a series of "rooms," each with a specific function and including the outdoor kitchen and a patio with hot tub.

"When you have such a large view site, you want to prevent a feeling of too much exposure," she explains. "This can be handled by creating smaller, more contained areas for people to congregate in, and which bring a feeling of intimacy to the space."

FACING LEFT: Low walls and elevation changes form small "rooms," a design technique that can prevent a large yard such as this from feeling too exposed. Surrounded by adobe-style walls, the kitchen area has an intimacy that might have been lost without the enclosure. The kitchen is located on the upper portion of the two-level patio.

FACING RIGHT: The walls of the kitchen enclosure resemble traditional adobe but are a more modern combination of stucco-clad concrete block. The seating benches are honed granite to match the kitchen counter, and the cabinet doors were crafted from a salvaged mesquite gate.

ABOVE: At several acres, the yard presented numerous opportunities for open-air living spaces, including this hot tub patio located next to the outdoor kitchen. The patio floor is Arizona flagstone and the retaining wall was constructed of local sandstone.

Kitchen and Fireplace in One

DESIGN: Pete Pedersen, Pedersen Associates

PHOTOGRAPHS: Laurence Bartone

LOCATION: *Atherton, California*

FEATURES: *cooking center and outdoor fireplace contained in a single unit*

KEY MATERIALS: *bluestone, cedar, glulam beams*

SPECIAL TOUCHES: *extra-large hearth at fireplace for seating, halogen lights on dining patio trellis, gas grill with rotisserie*

An outdoor kitchen performs double duty in this efficient design by landscape architect Pete Pedersen: one side houses the cooking center while the other reveals a wood-burning fireplace that acts as the focal point of the adjacent dining and seating patio.

With this project, Pedersen wasn't hindered by a lack of space, but his inventive kitchen station would work equally well in a more compact setting. "By giving the station two sides with independent functions, it doesn't intrude into the patio or yard," he says. "And, by facing the kitchen toward the patio, we made sure that the person doing the cooking wouldn't have to stand with his back to others."

Pedersen's clients wanted an outdoor entertainment area that would be able to accommodate adults and kids, and his site plan specified a pool and a large expanse of lawn (a "kid magnet," in the architect's words) in addition to the dining/seating patio and kitchen. Mature oak trees along the perimeter of the yard effectively screen views to a neighboring house and enhance privacy.

The interior rooms of the home transition to the outdoor spaces via a long patio clad in Connecticut bluestone pavers. The patio terminates at one end in an outdoor dining room protected by a sturdy trellis wired with halogen lights. Just steps from the dining area is the fireplace, a substantial structure with a wide hearth for seating. The kitchen side of the station includes a gas grill with rotisserie and side burner, ice maker, sink and wood storage.

LOCATION MATTERS

When deciding where to put your outdoor kitchen, keep in mind it's no fun for the cook to be isolated from everyone else. To solve this, face the kitchen toward the rest of the yard, or build a seating/dining counter into the kitchen station so that people can sit and talk to the chef.

The home opens to an expansive lawn, the perfect setting for an outdoor room complete with dining patio and adjacent kitchen/fireplace station.

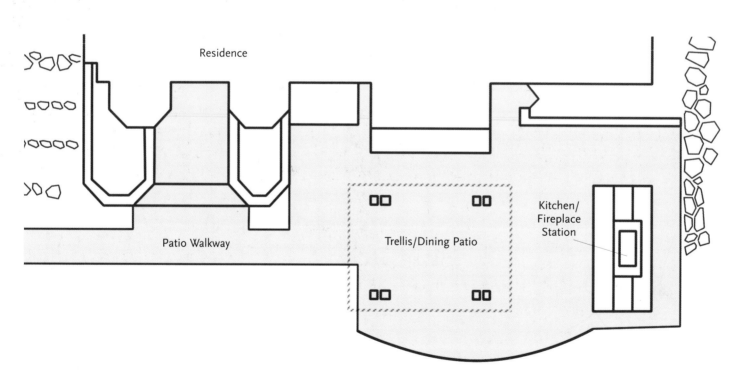

Residence

Patio Walkway

Trellis/Dining Patio

Kitchen/
Fireplace
Station

FACING: The interior rooms transition to the out-door living spaces with a long patio that can be accessed from several points inside the house. Low terrace walls made from San Francisco cobble create the illusion of a stone foundation.

ABOVE: Located just off the family room, the dining patio is protected by a sturdy trellis constructed of painted exterior-grade glulam beams and inset with a stained cedar lattice wired with small halogen lights. The patio pavers are Connecticut bluestone.

ABOVE: A substantial wood-burning fireplace fronts one side of the kitchen/fireplace station and is a welcoming place to gather for conversation and warmth. The station has a concrete block core and is clad in one-inch Connecticut bluestone veneer. The veneer gives the structure visual weight but is less expensive than stone block.

FACING: The kitchen side of the station reveals the efficiency of incorporating two elements into one unit. The kitchen's features include a built-in gas grill with rotisserie and side burner, a sink, an ice maker and wood storage. When no plants are on the ledge above the grill, the cook can easily see and interact with people in the seating and dining areas while preparing the food.

CREATIVE FUNCTIONALITY

Festive Backyard Retreat

DESIGN: Colleen Holmes, New Leaf Landscape

PHOTOGRAPHS: Kathlene Persoff

LOCATION: *North Hollywood, California*

FEATURES: *combined outdoor kitchen/living room with unusual decorative accents*

KEY MATERIALS: *rose quartz, amethyst quartz, Utah Ice stone, "candy stripe" flagstone, glass tile*

SPECIAL TOUCHES: *antique refrigerator and Azul Macuba kitchen counter*

This outdoor kitchen in North Hollywood inhabits a backyard room complete with fireplace, pool, waterfall, antique Coca-Cola refrigerator and life-size cast resin hippopotamus "rescued" from a regional zoo.

Revamped by landscape designer Colleen Holmes with plenty of input from the owner, the yard features a kaleidoscope of color and decorative accents that elicit a double take—for example, the hippopotamus and three plastic palm trees outfitted with fiber optic lighting (even the coconuts illuminate). Overall, the redo of the small L-shaped yard and existing pool brought a festive vacation-like atmosphere while maintaining privacy, important in this close-in neighborhood.

The new backyard design—including the kitchen—evolved from the focal point of a wood-burning fireplace, around which the owner has arranged outdoor furniture. Color and texture abound in the selections of stone, fabric and glass tile. Even the garden wall got a new coat of paint: a pale blue that is an unassuming backdrop for the more dramatic events taking place within. "My design theme was based on that magical twilight hour, as sunset approaches and the sky is full of color," Holmes says. "That's the mood we tried to capture here—that elevated state where you don't want the day to end. The point is to be happy when you are in the yard."

HOW'S THE VIEW?

Aesthetics are important when it comes to the design of an outdoor kitchen. How will it appear from inside the house? It should be eye-pleasing as well as functional.

It would be difficult not to smile at the yard's many whimsical and creative details, among them a wall mural with a sky that twinkles with fiber optic lights and a glass tile mosaic on the pool floor and walls. Although understated by comparison, the kitchen was built for function and equipped with a wood-burning barbecue, sink, refrigerator, ice maker and warming drawer.

Holmes' materials palette reflects the owner's near obsession with color. The patio stone resembles vanilla ice cream swirled with chocolate and strawberry. These "candy stripe" pavers are accented with pink Arizona flagstone, which in turn complements the rose quartz used on the kitchen and fireplace. The kitchen counter is a substantial slab of Azul Macuba, chosen for its hints of blue, teal and lavender.

The backyard is styled in the manner of an outdoor room, complete with kitchen and fireplace. The kitchen is plumbed for hot and cold running water and is equipped with durable, weather-resistant stainless steel appliances, including a barbecue, under-counter refrigerator, ice maker and warming drawer. The blue plastic palm tree is wired with fiber optic cable (even the coconuts light up), and the "candy stripe" patio pavers are in a vibrant pattern of pinks, creams and light browns.

FACING: The kitchen counter was crafted from Azul Macuba stone, here with a chiseled face edge. Both the kitchen surround and the fireplace showcase the natural beauty of rose quartz, amethyst quartz and Utah Ice stone.

ABOVE RIGHT: The cast resin hippopotamus was found at a regional zoo and now lives happily in the yard, and a red fiber optic palm tree brightens the pool patio. The garden walls were painted a pale blue for an understated backdrop to the high-spirited space.

BELOW RIGHT: The garage/guest house became the backdrop for an antique Coca-Cola refrigerator and a fitting place for a mural. The sky in the mural is outfitted with fiber optic pinpoint lights that at night can be turned on to produce a starry sky.

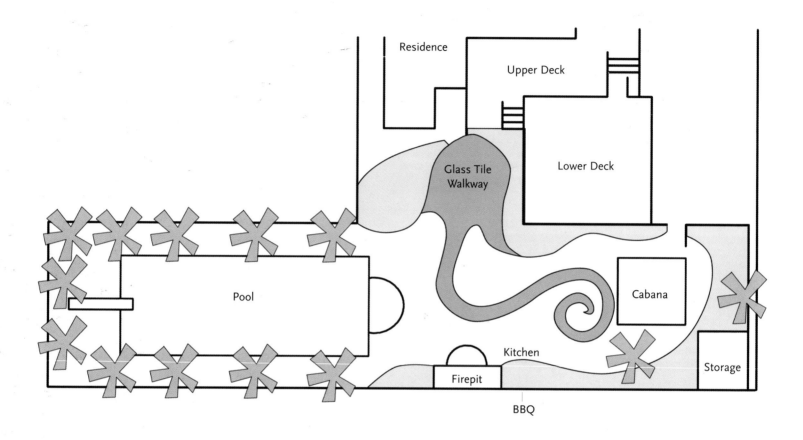

Residence

Upper Deck

Lower Deck

Glass Tile
Walkway

Pool

Cabana

Kitchen

Firepit

Storage

BBQ

FACING: The remodeled pool dazzles with a glass tile mosaic of hibiscus blossoms and tropical fish. The pool floor was updated with a polished marble finish, and the deck is rainbow slate. The waterfall at the far end of the pool is wired with fiber optic lighting that can be programmed to display a variety of colors.

Wine Bottle Redux

DESIGN: Scott Cohen, The Green Scene

PHOTOGRAPHS: Deidra Walpole and Nick Lucero

LOCATION: *Simi Valley, California*

FEATURES: *U-shaped kitchen with gas grill and under-counter refrigerator*

KEY MATERIALS: *cast concrete, cinder block, stucco*

SPECIAL TOUCHES: *wine bottle panels backlit with fiber optic cables, hand-painted porcelain tiles*

Designed for a pair of oenophiles who host frequent tasting parties in their backyard, this outdoor kitchen reveals how something old can be turned into something new and exciting—in this case, 330 used wine bottles stacked on top of each other to form kaleidoscopic panels backlit with fiber optic cables. The cables are connected to a color wheel and, as the wheel turns, it sends varying hues through the bottles for a striking visual effect.

The panels transformed the basic cinder block and stucco barbecue station into an artistic—and environmentally responsible—statement. Explains designer Scott Cohen, "The decorative nature of the wine bottles made them a natural accent for the kitchen design. And, the owners were able to showcase their love of wine in a way that added to the beauty of their home in a very dramatic way."

You might not think wine bottles would be durable enough for this kind of application, but it turns out they are surprisingly sturdy. Cohen, however, didn't leave anything to chance. "Working with our structural engineer, we developed a standard weight load for an average wine bottle," he explains. "They are actually quite strong—just about equal to building with the glass blocks typically used in glass wall construction."

Special effects aside, a well-functioning kitchen was important to the owners. The U-shaped layout provides ample standing room—for example, two people can work the grill and another can serve. Equipped with a gas grill, refrigerator and stainless steel storage drawers, the kitchen is an eye-catching place to gather for a glass of vino and an open-air dining experience.

LAYOUT BASICS

The scope of your outdoor kitchen will depend on your yard, budget and lifestyle, but make sure its layout is as efficient and comfortable as possible. A basic single galley island with a built-in grill can be turned into a double galley by placing another counter opposite, in a parallel configuration. An L-shaped kitchen provides connected counters for cooking and eating, and a U-shaped layout adds even more counter space, making it possible to install special appliances and reserve one counter for seating and dining.

The kitchen's cinder block base was covered in stucco to match the house, and its U-shaped layout is spacious enough to accommodate more than one cook. The kitchen is equipped with a gas grill, under-counter refrigerator and stainless steel storage drawers. The patio is stamped concrete with a texture that resembles real stone, and the stepping-stones are slate. *Photo by Deidra Walpole.*

ABOVE: With its kaleidoscopic arrangement of recycled wine bottles backlit with fiber optics, the kitchen station reflects the owners' passion for wine. Some 330 wine bottles were carefully stacked and grouted with cement and then outfitted with fiber optic cables that send shimmering light through the glass. The cast concrete counter is accented by a strip of hand-painted porcelain tile in a grapevine pattern. *Photo by Deidra Walpole.*

FACING: At night, the backlit panels are a colorful backdrop for outdoor wine-tasting parties. *Photo by Nick Lucero.*

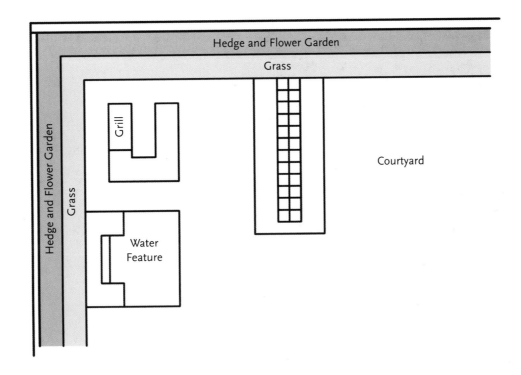

Hedge and Flower Garden

Grass

Hedge and Flower Garden

Grass

Grill

Water Feature

Courtyard

Slopeside Patio Dining

DESIGN: Bill Poss and Lyndal Williams, Poss Architecture, Planning & Interior Design

PHOTOGRAPHS: David O. Marlow and Patrick Sudmeier

LOCATION: *Aspen, Colorado*

FEATURES: *outdoor barbecue station and indoor fireplace designed as one connected unit*

KEY MATERIALS: *red sandstone, stained concrete, polished slate*

SPECIAL TOUCHES: *located slopeside for convenient ski-in/ski-out access*

It sounds irresistibly glamorous: ski a few runs, then pop in for a quick lunch before hitting the slopes again. Or, have dinner under the stars on a warm summer night. In reality it's a practical solution for the extended family that gathers at this slopeside vacation home for get-togethers and to enjoy the outdoorsy lifestyle of Aspen, Colorado.

Designed by architect Bill Poss and associate Lyndal Williams, the home is poised on a steep section of ski hill and steps down the site in seven levels in a configuration that made it possible to install a series of patios and decks for numerous outdoor living options. The dining/entertainment patio is located just off the indoor kitchen and living room on the fifth level and in an unusual twist on the outdoor kitchen concept, the barbecue is built right into the house—in fact, it is the back side of the living room fireplace, and the two share the same chimney stack. This creative design technique consolidated the barbecue and fireplace into one compact and connected unit, which in turn maximized the patio space. The grill sits in a red sandstone surround with a stained concrete base, colorful materials that complement the slate patio floor and the home's zinc, copper and cypress exterior.

The architects oriented the dining patio toward the south for maximum sun exposure, especially important during the winter season. While many outdoor kitchens and dining areas incorporate shade elements into their designs, this one welcomes as much sunshine as it can get—especially nice while catching a bite to eat before jumping back on the lift.

CLIMATE CONSIDERATIONS

Outdoor kitchens in locales with cooler year-round temperatures come with special considerations. For example, you might need a heat source—a fireplace, firepit or free-standing heater—to keep people warm. Plumbing systems must be carefully installed so that they don't freeze, and sinks will have to be drained when the kitchen is shut down and winterized.

The exterior of the home showcases a variety of materials, including painted copper cladding on the side bay window, cypress and zinc. A prime location on an Aspen ski hill made a ski-in/ski-out dining and entertainment patio equipped with a simple outdoor grill a smart and practical choice. The patio is oriented toward the south for maximum sun exposure. *Photo by David O. Marlow.*

FACING: The patio is partially enclosed by a red sandstone retaining wall and has a sealed and polished slate floor. A dining table and comfortable seating around the barbecue create the look of an outdoor room. *Photo by David O. Marlow.*

RIGHT: The barbecue station appears to emerge from the building and shares the same chimney stack as the living room fireplace. The grill is housed in a red sandstone surround with a stained concrete base. The unit is framed by windows that give the cook a view of the goings-on inside the house. *Photo by Patrick Sudmeier.*

BELOW: The flip side of the barbecue station is an indoor fireplace, also with a red sandstone surround. Clerestory windows inset with a fixed brise-soleil allow natural light to filter into the living room. *Photo by David O. Marlow.*

The patio is set up for meals under the stars.

Photo by Patrick Sudmeier.

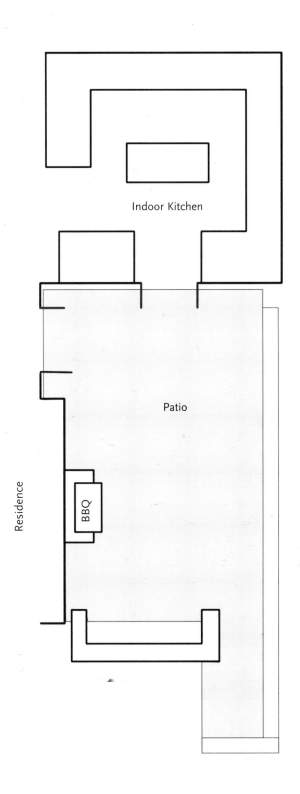

Indoor Kitchen

Patio

Residence

BBQ

The barbecue is located near the kitchen for an indoor/outdoor connection and accessed through cherry wood and glass doors. The proximity of the kitchen to the barbeque encourages people to circulate inside and out. *Photo by Patrick Sudmeier.*

Caribbean-Inspired Outdoor Space

DESIGN: Colleen Holmes, New Leaf Landscape

PHOTOGRAPHS: Robert Holmes

LOCATION: *Thousand Oaks, California*

FEATURES: *two-level bar/kitchen station with stainless steel grill and side burner*

KEY MATERIALS: *porcelain tile, flagstone, concrete*

SPECIAL TOUCHES: *Caribbean-style outbuilding, gas firepit*

Colorful and unique would aptly describe this outdoor kitchen-focused backyard created by landscape designer Colleen Holmes.

Before Holmes worked her magic on the half-acre site, it was "outdated, lacked visual interest and had too much hardscape. You could say there was very little curb appeal," she says. By adding a freestanding outdoor kitchen, embellishing the landscaping with additional plants, upgrading the existing pool with a waterfall and spa, and erecting a small Caribbean-style outbuilding, she gave the yard some much-needed pizzazz.

When contemplating the design and placement of the kitchen, Holmes chose to position it so that the cook could face the yard and thus be able to interact with others. A double-height counter combines bar seating and a prep counter in a single unit—a space-saving and budget-conscious technique. The kitchen is nicely equipped with a built-in gas grill and side burner, an under-counter refrigerator with ice maker, and storage drawers. The counters and backsplash are inlaid with porcelain tiles that match those on the pool, and the concrete block island is fronted with stacked veneer flagstone. Additional improvements to the property included new flagstone patio pavers, a side-yard seating area with fountain, and a gas firepit.

BEYOND THE GRILL

A basic grill is a necessity, but additional features can make cooking outdoors even more fun and efficient. For example, rotisseries can be prepped and started before guests arrive so that the food can cook largely unattended while the chef socializes. Side burners are useful for heating sauces, sautéing vegetables, quickly cooking fish and boiling water.

Privacy was achieved with a high retaining wall and tall perimeter plantings. The Caribbean-style outbuilding was given a corrugated metal roof, Dutch door and wood siding. The gas firepit is housed in a stacked veneer flagstone surround.

FACING: The double-height kitchen island faces the yard to allow the cook to interact with others while preparing the meal.

ABOVE: Equipped with a stainless steel gas grill and side burner, under-counter refrigerator with ice maker, and storage drawers, the kitchen illustrates how functionality and flair can coexist beautifully. The concrete block island is covered in stacked veneer flagstone, and the tiles match those on the pool.

FACING: A new spa flows into the pool, which has been updated with porcelain tiles in a variety of blues, yellows and light greens. The patio is flagstone.

BELOW: Previously an unused side yard, the new seating area is a quiet place to relax. The patio is economical concrete with a stamped slate pattern.

Compact and Colorful

DESIGN: William O'Dowd

PHOTOGRAPHS: Wayne Thom

LOCATION: *Redondo Beach, California*
FEATURES: *pull-out storage baskets, heated hot water at sink, food prep/buffet counter*
KEY MATERIALS: *terrazzo, glass tile, cedar, redwood, concrete*
SPECIAL TOUCHES: *custom etched-glass backsplash, outdoor lighting, sound system*

A plan for a bare-bones barbecue morphed into a full-fledged outdoor kitchen when owner/architect William O'Dowd realized how much fun it would be to have friends over to cook and dine alfresco. Located just three blocks from the Pacific Ocean in Redondo Beach, this galley-style kitchen reveals a design concept that merges functionality with unusual creative details that together give the space its character and individuality.

O'Dowd built his outdoor kitchen just off the indoor kitchen so that moving between the two would be as straightforward as possible. The stainless steel grill and side burner are housed in a terrazzo frame, and all the counters and work surfaces are terrazzo as well. He wanted a sink for quick clean-up, but wasn't content to use cold water to rinse the dishes. Instead, he hooked up the sink to a water heater hidden below the counter. A redwood and cedar trellis covers the kitchen and dining table and is a framework for outdoor lighting and a sound system.

Many outdoor kitchens include storage cabinets, some fronted with stainless steel and others with wood, but O'Dowd wanted something simpler. His solution? Wire baskets that slide in and out of niches in the barbecue station. The baskets keep supplies close at hand and require no maintenance—unlike wood cabinets, for example. In another "why cover it up?" move, the architect chose to hang pots and pans from the trellis rather than hide them from view.

"I wanted a kitchen built out of solid materials and set up so that everything would be within easy reach," he says. "The point was to combine convenience with a bit of fun. I think both goals were accomplished."

WHY A TRELLIS?

A trellis can provide excellent sun protection, but its function doesn't stop there. It can also serve as the framework for light fixtures and stereo speakers.

The long patio was able to accommodate an outdoor dining room and kitchen. A redwood and cedar trellis shades the patio and protects it from rain, and outdoor lighting on individual dimmer switches and a sound system help transform the patio into party central.

ABOVE: The kitchen's open galley layout allows the cook to move easily between the grill station and adjacent food prep/buffet counter, which is supported by three "legs" made from sewer pipe. The kitchen is equipped with a gas grill and side burner and a sink with hot running water.

LEFT: The backsplash is a custom blown glass panel engraved with a sea life motif and backlit for additional lighting at night.

FACING: The architect hung pots and pans from the trellis and opted for a simple basket storage system instead of traditional cabinets. The baskets can be pulled out to retrieve utensils, napkins, plates and other dining essentials and, unlike wood, require no maintenance. The barbecue frame and counters are durable terrazzo, and the glass tiles act as a colorful accent against the darker materials.

Indoor/Outdoor Kitchen Connection

DESIGN: Michelle Van de Voorde, Elemental Design Group

PHOTOGRAPHS: Gregory Case

LOCATION: *San Mateo, California*

FEATURES: *outdoor kitchen with a convenient "pass-through" orientation to the indoor kitchen*

KEY MATERIALS: *stainless steel, concrete, stucco, bluestone*

SPECIAL TOUCHES: *colored concrete apron around the kitchen station to set it apart from the rest of the yard*

This galley-style kitchen for a family that loves spending time outdoors has a straightforward indoor/outdoor connection thanks to a sliding window that allows food and other cooking and dining items to be passed easily between the house and the yard.

"Positioning the kitchen near the interior kitchen was the logical choice," says landscape architect Michelle Van de Voorde. "With this placement, it's easy to hand food back and forth without having to keep going in and out of the house."

The kitchen is just one component of a well-organized backyard that also includes a canopy-covered seating area, separate recreation terrace and dining patio. "The owners have an extended family that they like to invite over for gatherings, so their outdoor space needed work on a variety of levels, whether the focus was on cooking, entertaining, relaxing or playing," Van de Voorde explains.

GRILL OPTIONS

Grills are becoming increasingly fancy, so research your options before you purchase. Some come with trays that hold wood chips, which impart a smoky flavor to food, while others have grids that can be positioned at different heights above the heat source. Still others have motorized rotisseries for cooking whole roasts, chickens or turkeys.

The architect built the kitchen right up against the house, taking advantage of a deep overhang that offers some protection from the elements. A cast concrete counter tops the unit, which has been clad in stucco to match the house. Appliances include a gas grill and warming drawer and a double-sided under-counter refrigerator.

Used year-round, this open-air grill station proves that even the simplest of designs can be customized for maximum efficiency and convenience.

ABOVE: By placing the outdoor kitchen along the exterior wall of the indoor kitchen, the architect ensured that food prep and transferring items between inside and out would be as convenient as possible. The door to the right leads to the indoor kitchen.

RIGHT: Food and other dining items can be passed between the indoor and outdoor kitchens through a sliding window, and the proximity of the indoor sink omitted the need for one outside.

The refrigerator doors, warming drawer, grill cover and hood are all stainless steel, and the patio around the kitchen station is colored concrete with a bluestone border to complement the stone used on the dining and seating patios. The kitchen is protected from the elements by an overhang.

RIGHT: A long table adjacent to the kitchen turns backyard dining into a family affair.

BELOW LEFT: The kitchen is equipped with a stainless steel gas grill and warming drawer below. The unit is clad in stucco and has a cast concrete counter.

BELOW RIGHT: The kitchen's stainless steel storage cabinet (to the left) is fronted with painted tongue-in-groove wood panels. A double-sided under-counter refrigerator keeps drinks on hand and saves trips into the house for refills.

Whimsical "Martini" Bar

DESIGN: Scott Cohen, The Green Scene

PHOTOGRAPHS: Nick Lucero

LOCATION: *Porter Ranch, California*

FEATURES: *poolside outdoor kitchen with adjacent spa crafted to look like a martini glass*

KEY MATERIALS: *stucco, cast concrete, glass tile*

SPECIAL TOUCHES: *three-dimensional decorative tiles in the shapes of martini glasses, olives and bottles*

Equal parts suave and playful, this outdoor kitchen/bar adjoins a spa sculpted to resemble a martini glass. Did James Bond have anything to do with this?

Landscape designer Scott Cohen got the idea for the martini-themed entertainment space after attending one of the owners' martini parties. When they told him they wanted to do something with their bland dirt-floor backyard, he suggested they incorporate their love of all things martini right into the design. They agreed. One olive or two?

Cohen's first task was to remove the debris from a collapsed retaining wall and shore up the yard with new retaining walls and updated hardscape features, including a pool patio finished in stamped concrete. He poured a shapely free-form pool and then installed a kitchen/bar station equipped with a gas grill and drinks cooler. Tiled barstools built into the long side of the spa provide swim-up-to-the-counter seating, and the martini glass is outfitted with jets that pulsate water over sore backs and feet. Shaken or stirred?

Cohen gave the kitchen a bold stroke of color with a backsplash covered in handmade porcelain tiles in the shapes of martini glasses, olives and bottles. An experienced tile artisan and evidently a stickler for authenticity, he used a real martini glass and bottles to create molds for the tiles but he didn't stop there. He also used real olives for the olive molds, which resulted in tiles that look good enough to eat—or line up on a toothpick. The owners and their children got involved in the fun by helping to paint and glaze the tiles.

KITCHEN ZONES

Whether you opt for a freestanding or attached outdoor kitchen will depend on your yard and how you plan to use the kitchen. If you desire a "destination" within the yard, or a separate entertainment space, a freestanding structure might be your best option, budget permitting. If you want to keep the outdoor kitchen close to the house, you can place it against an exterior wall or a few steps from the building.

The fully remodeled backyard has a new patio and an integrated pool, spa and outdoor kitchen/bar entertainment area. The patio is stamped textured concrete and the pool coping is Arizona flagstone.

The twelve-foot-long spa terminates on one side in a "martini glass" covered in pearlescent tiles that shift color in the sun. The spa is equipped with massage jets and built-in seating along the counter side.

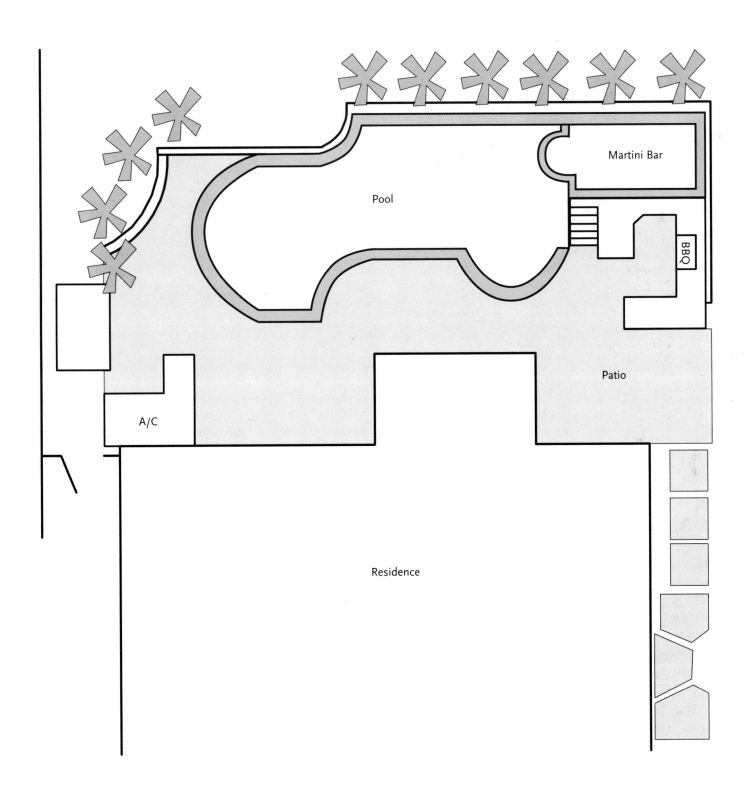

Pool

Martini Bar

BBQ

Patio

A/C

Residence

ABOVE: The kitchen/bar station has a cinder block core and was clad in stucco to match the house. Its simple layout provides plenty of room for a gas grill and drinks cooler (opposite the grill). The counters are cast concrete.

LEFT: The tiled backsplash adds a vivid decorative element to the kitchen.

The designer created tile molds using real bottles and olives and a martini glass from the owners' collection. The resulting three-dimensional porcelain tiles look as authentic as their inspiration. Blue glass tile chips form the backdrop.

Understated Kitchen/Pool Patio

DESIGN: Colleen Holmes, New Leaf Landscape

PHOTOGRAPHS: Robert Holmes

LOCATION: *Pacific Palisades, California*
FEATURES: *outdoor kitchen built against a substantial stone wall, gas firepit, pool*
KEY MATERIALS: *custom-cut Greek limestone, Jerusalem Gold stone, granite*
SPECIAL TOUCHES: *meditation fountain clad in glass tile, raised seating terrace*

For this hillside home in Pacific Palisades, landscape designer Colleen Holmes was given the challenge of not only outfitting the backyard with a kitchen and dining patio, but also finding a way to create a cohesive outdoor room.

With clear views to Santa Monica Bay and the Pacific Ocean, the yard didn't lack beautiful scenery. It did lack a layout that made sense; according to Holmes, the problems began at the front door. "The house didn't have a proper entry," she explains. "We fixed that by creating a series of spaces that culminate in the backyard—now you enter the front door and go into a hall that leads to a courtyard and from there follows to the yard."

As the work progressed, the outdoor kitchen became a key part of the yard. Equipped with a gas grill and side burner, refrigerator with ice maker, and warming drawer, it is built into a stone retaining wall topped with a pergola. A precast concrete wood-burning fireplace anchors the kitchen and keeps the dining patio warm during cool weather, and a granite counter extends from the grill for a casual place to sit and enjoy a meal.

Also central to the design was an existing pool, remodeled with blue glass tiles and limestone coping and just steps from a seating terrace that includes a gas firepit for warmth and weather-resistant teak furniture. The designer raised the terrace two feet above the yard to capture the views and gently separate it from the rest of the yard. The tranquil mood of this outdoor room is enhanced with several water features, among them a meditation fountain clad in hand-cut glass tiles and flanked by tall feathery grasses.

The primary materials, understated to allow the scenery and landscaping to shine, include custom-cut Greek limestone, in some places with a chiseled face edge and in others a honed finish, and Jerusalem Gold stone with a chiseled face.

"The design of this outdoor kitchen and the rest of the yard is really pretty simple," Holmes says. "But everywhere you turn, you see something special. The entire space has a very harmonious feel to it."

MAKE IT EASY

Pay attention to things that might seem obvious but if ignored can turn outdoor cooking into a chore. For example, how far will you have to reach or walk to set down a plate of hot food? You don't want to have to traipse all over the place searching for a free counter, so make sure your design incorporates ample counter space right next to the grill.

The front entry is now more organized and inviting. The custom-cut Greek limestone patio has been inset with strips of grass for a softening effect, and the designer added a color enhancer and sealer to the limestone to bring out its warmer tones and to complement the Jerusalem Gold stone walls. The front door opens to a private courtyard that leads to the outdoor kitchen and the rest of the yard.

The outdoor kitchen, conveniently equipped with a gas grill, side burner, refrigerator with ice maker, and warming drawer, is placed up against a retaining wall clad in Jerusalem Gold stone and capped with a wood pergola, which over time will support jasmine and wisteria vines. The wood-burning fireplace is precast concrete to reflect the limestone patio, and the granite counter that extends from the grill provides a comfortable place to sit and eat. The glass window niches flanking the fireplace are wired for lighting.

ABOVE: One of three water features on the property, the meditation fountain, clad in hand-cut glass tiles and framed in Greek limestone, buffers noise from a nearby street. The grasses on either side of the fountain are *cyperus papyrus*.

FACING: The pool, located next to the seating terrace, is clad in light blue glass tiles.

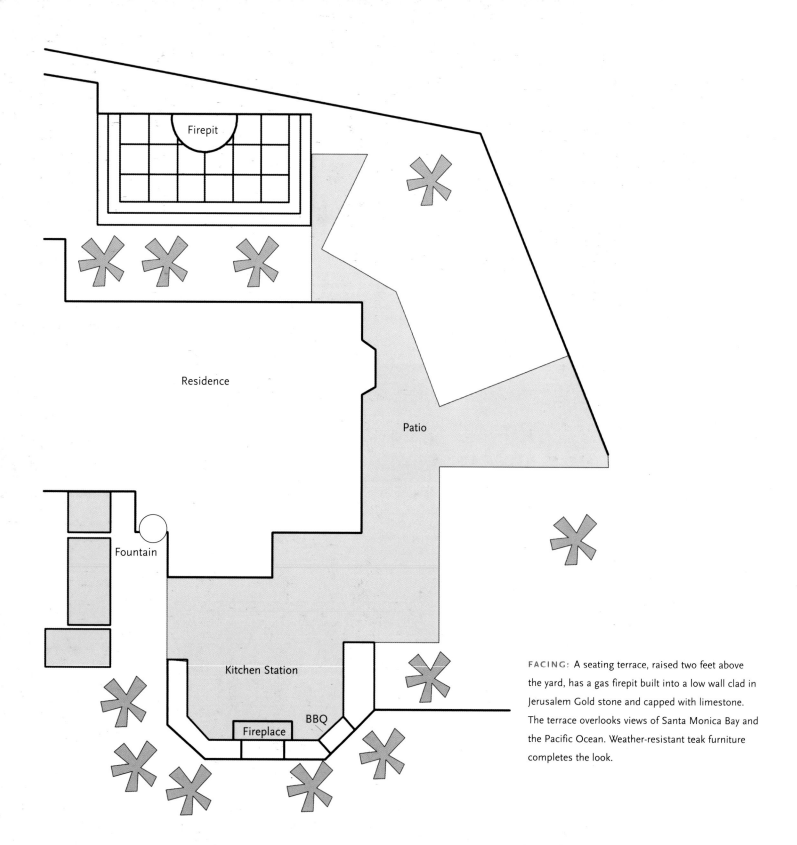

Firepit

Residence

Patio

Fountain

Kitchen Station

Fireplace

BBQ

FACING: A seating terrace, raised two feet above the yard, has a gas firepit built into a low wall clad in Jerusalem Gold stone and capped with limestone. The terrace overlooks views of Santa Monica Bay and the Pacific Ocean. Weather-resistant teak furniture completes the look.

Hamptons Summer Kitchen

DESIGN: Hugh Huddleson

PHOTOGRAPHS: Mark Samu

LOCATION: *East Hampton, New York*
FEATURES: *breezeway barbecue station adjacent to poolside kitchen building*
KEY MATERIALS: *brick, granite, cedar*
SPECIAL TOUCHES: *tiered shelf/storage system, trellis for shade*

The breezeway connecting two poolside buildings became the ideal place for a built-in barbecue station at this East Hampton summer home.

The buildings, with their cedar shingle exteriors and crisp white windows and doors, correspond to the modified Shingle-style architecture and materiality of the main house. One of the buildings is a changing area and shower, the other a full kitchen. The barbecue station sits opposite the kitchen in an arrangement of indoor/outdoor space that translates into a flexible environment for entertaining: food prep and cooking can be done right at the patio, and the proximity of the barbecue to the dining table and pool keeps the cook in close contact with others.

Architect Hugh Huddleson chose materials that age well—brick, granite, cedar—and require little, if any, maintenance. Positioned on axis with the pool, the breezeway is framed by a trellis crafted from cedar left in its natural state. In time, trailing vines will grow over the trellis, providing shade and bringing additional color to the patio.

The barbecue station itself is a beautiful complement to this elegant outdoor room. A stainless steel gas grill sits in a surround of intricate brickwork. Granite slabs form counters on either side of the grill and intersect the brick to form storage shelves and niches.

Huddleson aimed to make the barbecue a "noteworthy and central character in the pool area, one that would encourage people to congregate and enjoy the summer days and evenings."

HIRE A PRO

Although some outdoor kitchens resemble their indoor counterparts in terms of layout and appliances, outdoor kitchens have their own particular requirements—weather, which materials will last over time, how to set up plumbing lines and electricity, and how the kitchen fits in with the rest of the yard. When it comes to these kinds of details, the safest bet is to consult a design professional or architect.

On axis with the pool for an orderly presentation, the breezeway connects the changing room/shower (left) and poolside indoor kitchen (right). The pool deck is bluestone, which is not so bright as to necessitate sunglasses but not so dark that it becomes too hot for bare feet.

FACING: The architect chose a modest palette of materials, including cedar, brick and granite, that will age well and require little to no upkeep. The cedar used for the trellis was left in its natural state for a simple, maintenance-free look. In time, vines will cover the trellis, providing additional shade. The barbecue station is located in the breezeway, opposite the indoor kitchen and positioned so that the cook can interact with others while preparing the food.

ABOVE: The kitchen building has a clear view of the pool patio.

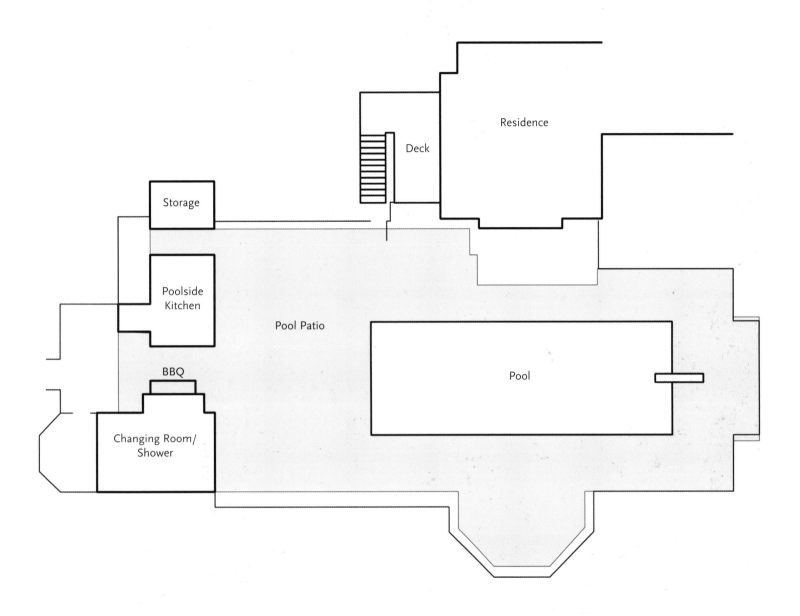

Residence

Deck

Storage

Poolside
Kitchen

Pool Patio

Pool

BBQ

Changing Room/
Shower

FACING: Elegant brickwork elevates this barbecue station beyond the everyday. Slabs of granite extend from either side of the grill to form counters and, below, intersect the brick to create a compact shelf/storage niche system.

GOING ALL OUT

A Taste of Tuscany

DESIGN: Scott Cohen, The Green Scene

PHOTOGRAPHS: Deidra Walpole

LOCATION: *Calabasas, California*

FEATURES: *kitchen and dining patio adjacent to dramatic vine-covered pergola*

KEY MATERIALS: *stone veneer, cast concrete, Douglas fir*

SPECIAL TOUCHES: *two-level counter at kitchen for added work space*

COUNTER LOGIC

Counters come in a variety of materials. Non-porous granite is heat- and weather-resistant but can be costly. Nonetheless, its longevity might make it worth the expense in the long-term. Budget-friendly ceramic tile is available in many colors and sizes, but grout can be problematic if it is not sealed properly. Weather-resistant concrete counters have the advantage of being grout-free and can be tinted to meet your color palette. They, too, can be pricey. Stainless steel also works well in outdoor settings and is particularly good for damp coastal environments. Soapstone, the material commonly associated with lab counters, is another option, but note that it is softer and therefore not as scratch-resistant as granite or other stone. It is, however, less expensive. In general, avoid wood counters for outdoor use because over time they will deteriorate under exposure to the sun and wet or cold weather.

With its extensive stone work, lush greenery and vine-covered pergola, this southern California backyard feels like a little slice of Italy.

Designer Scott Cohen's clients wanted their outdoor living space to exude a Tuscan ambience, and he responded with a landscape that looks as if it has been there for years. "By using lots of stone and being careful not to add too many hardscape features, we were able to provide the rustic feel the clients wanted," he says. "They weren't interested in anything modern-looking in terms of materials, but they did want modern conveniences."

Such conveniences are evident in the L-shaped kitchen, with its generous counter space, gas grill, side burner, refrigerator and proximity to a circular dining patio. The kitchen/dining area forms one of the "rooms" in the yard—Cohen suggested to his clients that individual zones connected by stepping-stone paths set into the grass would help define the yard and create mini destinations within it. The yard's other rooms are a trellised seating area oriented toward a wood-burning fireplace and a combination pool/spa.

The focal point of the yard is a freestanding vine-covered pergola constructed of Douglas fir that has been primed and painted to match the trim on the house. As beautiful as it is, the pergola serves a key role beyond the aesthetic: it effectively screens views to houses just beyond the yard. The pergola, which supports lush flowering trumpet vines, is an attractive way to maintain privacy in a close-in neighborhood and an elegant alternative to a solid wall.

Covered in flowering trumpet vines, the freestanding Douglas fir pergola screens views of neighboring houses and brings a touch of Tuscan-inspired styling to the property. Shown here around the pool and spa, concrete stepping-stones link the individual zones of the yard, which has been divided into distinct "rooms," including a kitchen/dining patio and a seating area with fireplace.

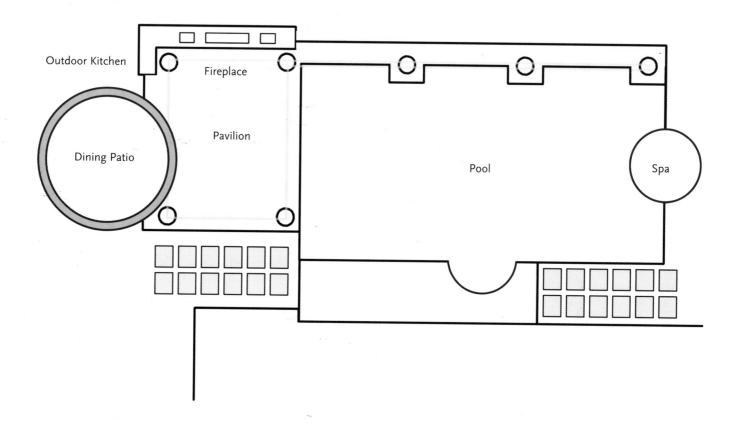

Outdoor Kitchen

Fireplace

Pavilion

Dining Patio

Pool

Spa

FACING: The wood-burning fireplace at the seating patio features cinder block construction with a stacked ledge stone veneer. The center firebox is flanked on either side by wood storage openings, and the hearth and mantel are cast concrete. The trellis helps to shade the patio.

FACING: The circular dining patio is raised above the lawn to visually separate it from the rest of the yard. The colored pavers in the center are tumbled concrete and the perimeter band is cast-in-place concrete with a bullnose step.

ABOVE: The L-shaped kitchen has a cinder block core and a stacked ledge stone veneer exterior to match the fireplace. Although the owners wanted a rustic design, they opted for modern stainless steel appliances, including a gas grill, side burner and under-counter refrigerator, as well as a storage cabinet. The counters provide plenty of work space and can accommodate buffet-style meals.

LEFT: The cast concrete kitchen counters were embedded with pieces of recycled glass for added color.

Fully Equipped Kitchen Pavilion

DESIGN: Ed Eubanks and Michael Dreef, Eubanks Group Architects

PHOTOGRAPHS: Filippo Castore

LOCATION: *Houston, Texas*

FEATURES: *cooking line with smoker, wood-fired barbecue, gas grill, commercial-grade vent hood*

KEY MATERIALS: *Texas cream limestone and brick with copper and mahogany accents*

SPECIAL TOUCHES: *European antiques, exercise room for working off the calories*

This open-air kitchen pavilion for a couple living on the outskirts of Houston, Texas, is the perfect setting for everything from fund-raising events and weddings to football parties and impromptu dinners.

Architects Ed Eubanks and Michael Dreef designed the pavilion to reflect the style and materiality of the main house, an updated French country–style dwelling. Sited as the focal point in the two-acre yard, the elevated 1,200-square-foot structure is accessed by low steps that set it apart from the rest of the property. Both the house and the pavilion have a toned-down materiality of brick and Texas cream limestone, slate (for each roof), and mahogany and copper accents.

The pavilion is spacious enough for an exercise room and bathroom and is filled with antiques from France and Italy. The kitchen features include a gas grill with rotisserie, side burner, smoker and wood-fired barbecue pit, all arranged in a cooking line against one wall. An under-counter refrigerator, ice maker and copper farm sink occupy the opposite wall.

POWER UP

Designers caution that many people underestimate how many electrical outlets they need for their outdoor kitchens. In addition to outlets for powering a gas grill, rotisserie or side burner, you might need extra outlets for a refrigerator, blender, food processor, coffee maker, etc.

The pavilion's limestone patio is inset with a fountain that also serves as a wading pool for the owners' grandchildren. The limestone balustrade, an antique from nineteenth-century France, has been capped with a limestone counter for a place to sit and take in the gardens. The antique iron lanterns on either side of the arch were converted to gas, and dark mahogany windows complement the limestone.

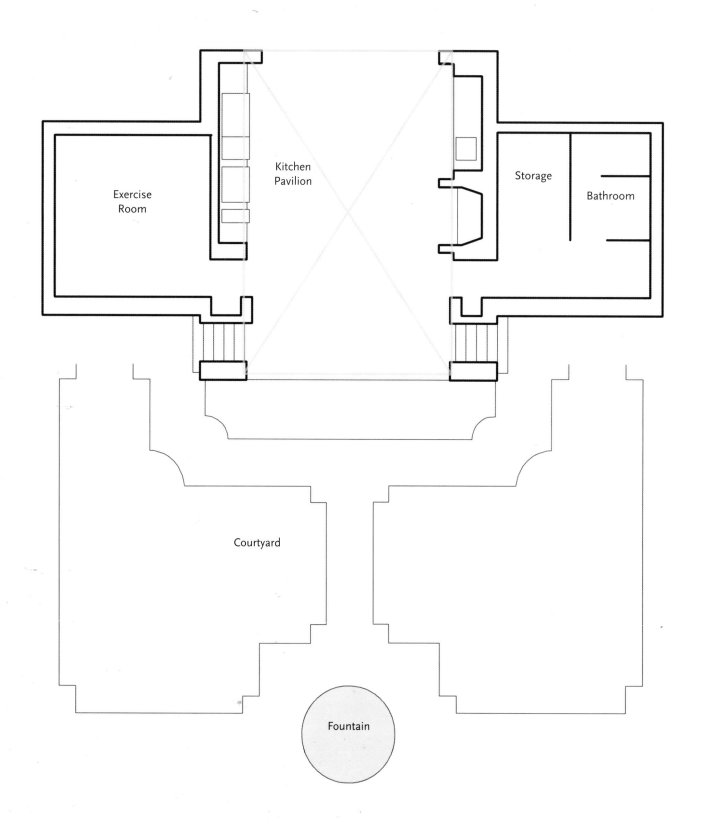

Exercise Room

Kitchen Pavilion

Storage

Bathroom

Courtyard

Fountain

ABOVE: The appliances in the cooking line make the kitchen a one-stop place to cook and entertain. From the left: a side burner, gas grill with rotisserie, and custom combination smoker/wood-fired barbecue pit. The interior walls are brick and limestone to reflect the materials of the main house.

RIGHT: A variety of woods can be used in the smoker to impart exotic flavors to foods—think pecan, hickory, mesquite and apple. The smoker uses indirect heat: wood is placed into the stainless steel–fronted cabinet directly below the unit. Heat and smoke intensity are controlled by manipulating the dampers at the fire-box and chimney.

FACING: The kitchen's exhaust system is contained within a standing seam copper canopy attached to a wood frame. The floor is limestone.

ABOVE: The arrangement of furniture gives the pavilion the feel of an open-air living room, and the dramatic arch frames views of the main house. The table in the foreground is nineteenth-century Italian marble. The mahogany door leads to the exercise room.

Rooftop Kitchen on the Beach

DESIGN: Ted Tokio Tanaka, Ted Tokio Tanaka Architects

PHOTOGRAPHS: Claudio Santini

LOCATION: *Marina Del Rey, California*
FEATURES: *rooftop outdoor living room with kitchen and dining area*
KEY MATERIALS: *stucco, glass, Trex decking, granite, stainless steel*
SPECIAL TOUCHES: *expandable fabric shade canopy*

Architect Ted Tokio Tanaka faced a special challenge when he was asked to convert two side-by-side beachfront condominiums in Marina Del Rey, California, into a single-family home. The twist? He had designed the condos twenty years earlier.

Tanaka's intimate knowledge of the buildings gave him an advantage as he embarked on the project, which he admits required "big surgery." The result is a family-oriented home just steps from the beach and one that frames ocean views at every turn.

Given the mild southern California climate, an outdoor room with a kitchen made perfect sense, but the yard was practically nonexistent—in fact, the building's footprint consumes most of the narrow lot. Ever the visionary, Tanaka trained his focus upward toward the newly combined rooftop decks that together added 1,500 square feet of outdoor living potential.

Tanaka arranged the deck into well-defined zones: one for the kitchen, one for the dining table, yet another for a living room–style arrangement of furniture, and one that is just the right size for a single lounge chair. He selected materials that are apropos to the beach vernacular and that will hold up to the coastal climate: crisp white stucco in a smooth finish, green glass, stainless steel and weather-resistant Trex decking.

Outfitted with only a gas grill and sink, the kitchen is simple and streamlined. Tanaka tucked it into a corner of the deck and used painted wood for the surround and granite for the counter. The next step was figuring out a way to protect diners and loungers from the sun. Tanaka came up with an ingenious way to shade the deck: an expandable accordion canopy made from sail fabric. The canopy stretches out along steel cables and doesn't encroach on the space as traditional garden umbrellas might have done. He addressed the need for wind protection with a glass panel that does its job without blocking the views.

The architect connected two side-by-side condominium units to form a single-family home. The 1,500-square-foot rooftop deck was turned into an outdoor living room with a kitchen and dining area. The dominant exterior material is white stucco in a smooth finish.

FACING: Trailing vines on the walls help soften the space, and Trex decking is a wise choice for a coastal climate because it can tolerate temperature and humidity fluctuations.

The deck is inset with a glass flooring panel that allows natural light into the master bedroom below and brings an eye-catching detail to the overall design. An expandable shade canopy made from sail fabric is an elegant and space-saving alternative to traditional patio umbrellas. The canopy originates at the dining table wall and can be stretched out along steel cables to shade a considerable portion of the deck.

FACING ABOVE: Tucked into a corner of the deck, the minimalist kitchen is equipped with a gas grill and sink set into a painted wood surround topped with a Brazilian Blue granite counter.

FACING BELOW: Windows on the kitchen wall bring sunlight into an interior staircase.

ABOVE: A glass panel offers wind protection without blocking views. The guardrail is painted stainless steel.

Deluxe Dining and Entertaining

DESIGN: Scott Cohen, The Green Scene

PHOTOGRAPHS: Deidra Walpole and Nick Lucero

LOCATION: *Calabasas, California*
FEATURES: *connected kitchen and spa, roll-out gas grill for flexible cooking options*
KEY MATERIALS: *cast concrete, ceramic tile, stone*
SPECIAL TOUCHES: *fiber optic lighting, beverage/condiment center*

This southern California backyard is a true outdoor entertainment room complete with kitchen station, seating and buffet counter, covered patio with fireplace, pool, spa and pond with fountain. The work of landscape designer Scott Cohen, the yard is sectioned into zones, a technique that works well for larger properties with multiple features and functions. "People naturally tend to break into groups and move around in clusters," he says. "It's important to create a sense of purpose in the yard, so that people are encouraged to move from zone to zone. You want them to take full advantage of what the garden has to offer."

Indeed, this yard has plenty to offer, including a galley kitchen with a food prep/dining counter and an adjacent bar-height seating/buffet counter. Although it looks built-in, the grill is on wheels and can be pulled out and moved to another section of the yard, if desired. The kitchen is also equipped with a sink and a beverage/condiment center.

Cohen constructed the kitchen and spa as a continuous unit, which allows those in the spa to stand at the counter and enjoy a drink or plate of food. Combining the kitchen and spa in this manner had the added benefit of maximizing patio space and, from a design perspective, integrated the two structurally and gave them a common materiality.

The materials in the kitchen mirror those used elsewhere in the yard, such as light-colored stone on the cinder block surround and ceramic tiles on the backsplash. The cast concrete counters are wired with fiber optic lighting that makes gatherings all the more celebratory.

FACING: The kitchen was designed so that the cook can work while guests are seated at the opposite bar counter, which is shaded by a palapa grass umbrella. *Photo by Deidra Walpole.*

ABOVE: The yard is organized into zones, all with a focus on entertaining. Guests can relax on the covered patio and enjoy the warmth of the fireplace and the sound of the adjacent fountain. The fireplace has a prefab stainless steel firebox and a cast concrete mantel. Concrete pads form a "floating" walkway across the water. *Photo by Deidra Walpole.*

FACING: The kitchen and spa are housed in a continuous unit. The designer used light-colored stone and ceramic tile around the spa and in the kitchen area. *Photo by Deidra Walpole.*

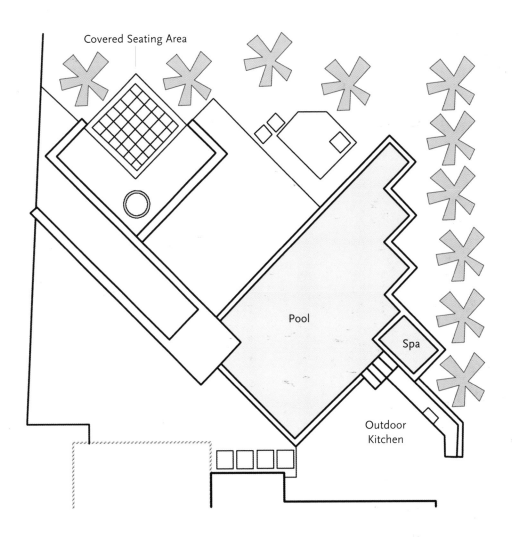

Covered Seating Area

Pool

Spa

Outdoor Kitchen

KEEP IT CLEAN

Plan for no-fuss clean-up when selecting counters. In general, the smoother the surface, the easier it will be to clean. Grout lines can trap food particles and stain if not finished and sealed properly. One popular counter option is smooth cast concrete, which can be sealed to prevent staining and cleans up with a simple swipe of a sponge.

FACING: Instead of being built into the kitchen station, the gas grill is on wheels, which gives the owners the option of moving it to another part of the patio. The cast concrete counters have been sealed to prevent staining, and the backsplash is decorated in ceramic tile. *Photo by Deidra Walpole.*

ABOVE: Fiber optic lighting at the kitchen counter lends drama to nighttime parties. The designer also placed lights beneath the edge of the counter to enhance the effect. *Photo by Nick Lucero.*

Sleek California Modernism

DESIGN: Steven Ehrlich, Steven Ehrlich Architects

PHOTOGRAPHS: Tim Street-Porter, Julius Shulman, David Glomb

LOCATION: *Santa Monica, California*
FEATURES: *indoor/outdoor entertainment pavilion with bar counter/kitchenette and attached outdoor barbecue station*
KEY MATERIALS: *concrete, stainless steel*
SPECIAL TOUCHES: *sliding glass panels at the pavilion that can be opened or closed, for flexible entertainment options*

Remodeling an existing house is challenge enough, but when the house in question is a historic landmark, the task suddenly becomes all the more daunting.

Architect Steven Ehrlich handled this project—the restoration of early California modernist Richard Neutra's 1938 Lewin residence followed by an addition that incorporates an attached entertainment pavilion—with a great deal of creativity and respect for the architect who came before him. "I felt it was important to relate the pavilion to Neutra's design, but not mimic it," Ehrlich explains. "The pavilion honors the original house but proclaims its own identity. The task was to make it a place for the new millennium, and in doing so hopefully make Neutra proud."

The house, which overlooks the Pacific Ocean, sits at the base of a bluff, just off the Pacific Coast Highway. Wanting to expand both their indoor and outdoor square footage, the current owners purchased a vacant lot next door and then put Ehrlich to work. The result is an addition to the back of the house and an indoor/outdoor pavilion that runs parallel to the house and opens to the yard, which has been updated with a new pool and barbecue station.

Echoing Neutra's proclivity for fusing interior and exterior space, three walls of the pavilion consist of floor-to-ceiling glass. The glass at each end of the building can slide completely away into a pocket between two concrete walls. Expanding on this theme of transparency, Ehrlich attached the pavilion to the house with an airy glass connector accessible from the dining room.

The stainless steel barbecue station extends from the pavilion's bar/kitchenette counter and is contained within a concrete frame. The station is equipped with a gas grill, refrigerator, ice maker and sink.

Designed by Richard Neutra in 1938, the house has been restored and updated with an indoor/outdoor entertainment pavilion, attached barbecue station, and pool. *Photo by Tim Street-Porter.*

ABOVE: With its stainless steel cycloidal arch and minimalist appearance, the entertainment pavilion echoes the design and materiality of the house but stands as an individual entity. The glass at both ends of the pavilion can slide away into pockets between two concrete walls, opening the room to the barbecue/pool patio and surrounding lawn. The house and pavilion are linked by a glass connector. *Photo by Tim Street-Porter.*

FACING: Perforated stainless steel on the pavilion ceiling absorbs sound, and the concrete floor and side wall give the building a substantial feel. The pavilion can be used year-round thanks to its sliding glass panels, which can close off the space during cooler weather. *Photo by Julius Shulman and David Glomb.*

ABOVE: The stainless steel outdoor barbecue station extends from the pavilion's bar/kitchenette. Housed in a solid concrete frame, it includes a gas grill, refrigerator, ice maker and sink. Stainless steel is a long-lasting choice for coastal environments. *Photo by Tim Street-Porter.*

FACING: The dining room opens to the glass connector joining the house to the pavilion. *Photo by Tim Street-Porter.*

Spacious Poolside Kitchen and Bar

DESIGN: Kevin Cunningham, Ultimate Outdoor Kitchen Company
PHOTOGRAPHS: Carola Kates

LOCATION: *Chicago, Illinois*
FEATURES: *double-sided kitchen/bar island with curved seating/serving counter*
KEY MATERIALS: *granite, stainless steel, concrete*
SPECIAL TOUCHES: *wine grotto, beer tap, double sinks and grills, fiber optic lighting*

If your ideal outdoor cooking situation involves being able to wine and dine a long list of guests in style, take your cues from this outdoor kitchen/bar island designed by Kevin Cunningham for a Chicago couple who think nothing of throwing a party for a hundred or more people. With everything from double grills and sinks to a beer tap and wine grotto, the island has the proper accoutrements for large-scale cooking and entertaining alfresco.

Although they had the advantage of a roomy backyard, Cunningham's clients didn't want their kitchen to consume too much space. He responded with a semi-enclosed kitchen/bar island that can simultaneously accommodate bartenders and cooks. The kitchen side of the island backs up against the upper pool terrace retaining wall and is in a straight line so that appliances, including two grills, are grouped together for maximum efficiency. The bar side of the island features a curving two-tiered seating/serving counter and includes an ice maker, refrigerator, twenty-five-bottle wine grotto and beer tap, also in a streamlined layout. All of the island's vertical and horizontal surfaces are granite in a color that plays off the exterior of the house.

Finally, although the kitchen already had a significant "wow" factor, Cunningham jazzed up things even more with fiber optic lighting at the island and pool.

LIGHT SHOWS

Fiber optic cables are a savvy choice for outdoor lighting because they can withstand all kinds of weather without breaking down. And, they can be programmed to create impressive light shows right in your backyard. A nice fiber optic setup will cost around $2,000 to $3,000. Another benefit: fiber optic systems are inexpensive to run.

A concrete railing serves as a backdrop to the kitchen side of the island, enhancing the feeling of enclosure without blocking views to the upper pool terrace.

LEFT: The layout of the kitchen/bar island makes it possible to serve drinks and prepare food at the same time, and the curved counter provides plenty of seating for guests. The principal material on the island is granite.

BELOW LEFT: The kitchen side of the island is designed to handle big outdoor parties. It includes two gas grills, an under-counter refrigerator, storage and warming drawers, and a double-bowl sink.

BELOW RIGHT: The bar side of the island is equipped with a double-bowl sink, under-counter refrigerator, ice maker, beer tap and twenty-five-bottle wine grotto.

FACING: Fiber optic lighting around the island and pool turns evening gatherings into special events.

Kitchen Patio for Day and Night

DESIGN: Scott Cohen, The Green Scene

PHOTOGRAPHS: Nick Lucero

LOCATION: *Oak Park, California*

FEATURES: *split-level counter design, gas grill with rotisserie, refrigerator*

KEY MATERIALS: *cast concrete, glass tile, stucco-clad cinder block core*

SPECIAL TOUCHES: *fiber optic lighting, separate pool/spa patio with wood-burning fireplace*

Creative lighting gives this outdoor kitchen the ability to transition seamlessly from day to night.

Designed by Scott Cohen for a client who loves to throw parties, the kitchen is one component of a remodeled backyard that went from no-frills to functional. It reads like an extension of the house because Cohen was careful to make it look and feel like an outdoor room.

This technique isn't new to Cohen, who recommends that large yards be sectioned off into individual zones, a design concept that encourages people to move around rather than stay in one spot. He achieved that goal here by making the kitchen patio a destination within the yard, an effect that was further enhanced with the addition of a wood trellis covering. Guests can gather around the kitchen or mingle on the adjacent pool patio. "The objective is to inspire people to experience the yard in its entirety, versus just a piece of it," Cohen explains.

The kitchen features a practical split-level counter: the top level terminates in a round table raised to a bar-height of forty-six inches, while the lower level provides work space next to the grill. This all-in-one layout kept the footprint of the structure as compact as possible, and also facilitates interaction between the cook and those seated at the counter.

Proximity to the indoor kitchen made it possible to keep appliances to a minimum—a gas grill with rotisserie, under-counter refrigerator, and sink rounded out the picture nicely. Cohen used restraint with the color palette and materials, opting for a toned-down stucco veneer, cast concrete counters embedded with chunks of recycled glass, and a narrow band of glass tiles.

And, with the flick of a switch, fiber optic lights at the kitchen and pool patios can create an instant party mood—even the counter was given the opportunity to dazzle. "At night, the kitchen really lets its hair down," Cohen points out.

SAFETY CONSIDERATIONS

Extra safety precautions must be taken into account if you cover your kitchen with a wood trellis or other potentially flammable shelter. Make sure the covering is high enough to avoid becoming a fire hazard. If you have a gas grill, position the trellis fifty-four to sixty inches above it and, if you are using a charcoal or wood grill, plan for at least sixty inches of clearance.

Covered with a wood trellis to convey the look and feel of an outdoor room, the kitchen has a split-level design that contains work surfaces and a seating counter within a single structure. The designer downplayed the daytime appearance of the kitchen by cladding its cinder block core in stucco in a neutral color. The patio is stamped textured concrete.

ABOVE: A rounded bar-height counter extends from the cooking area in an orientation that promotes interaction between guests and the person working the grill.

FACING: The cast concrete counters have been embedded with chunks of recycled glass.

ABOVE: Fiber optic lighting wired into the counter, along with light fixtures installed beneath the edge of the counter and suspended from the trellis, transform the kitchen at night.

FACING: The pool patio has a spa and a wood-burning fireplace with a built-in backrest. Fiber optics around the pool complement the lighting in the kitchen.

Fresh Air and Beautiful Views

DESIGN: Ed Eubanks and Dale Dibello, Eubanks Group Architects

PHOTOGRAPHS: Filippo Castore

LOCATION: *Houston, Texas*

FEATURES: *protected open-air design, streamlined kitchen with gas grill, three-sided fireplace*

KEY MATERIALS: *English pine, mahogany, soapstone*

SPECIAL TOUCHES: *molded brick, louvered privacy window*

A lush natural setting provided the inspiration for this graceful open-air kitchen/living room in Houston, Texas.

Designed by architects Ed Eubanks and Dale Dibello for a couple with a passion for the outdoors, the 400-square-foot room frames views of a pine forest and small lake and offers protection from sun, rain and wind. "We chose to expose the space to the setting rather than close it off, so that the structure would embrace this great yard," Dibello explains. "The open walls provide both shelter and ventilation, and they give you the sense of being outdoors—but with a solid roof over your head."

Convenience was important to the owners, who didn't want to trek back and forth between the house and outdoor kitchen. The architects responded by incorporating the open-air kitchen right into the architecture of the house. Positioned just a few steps from the interior kitchen and breakfast room, the open-air kitchen is a true extension of the house, both in design and materiality.

The owners opted for a single-counter cooking area with a built-in gas grill and side burner, and extra counter space for food preparation and presentation. A three-sided brick fireplace provides warmth in chilly weather and visually anchors the space.

Located just beyond the indoor kitchen and breakfast room, the open-air kitchen reflects the English Tudor style of the main house, with its steeply pitched gable roof and brick exterior. Other materials include mahogany (doors and windows), copper (gutters and downspouts) and composition shingle roof tiles that resemble slate.

A three-sided brick fireplace is the focal point of the room. At 400 square feet, the space is big enough for a kitchen counter and seating area.

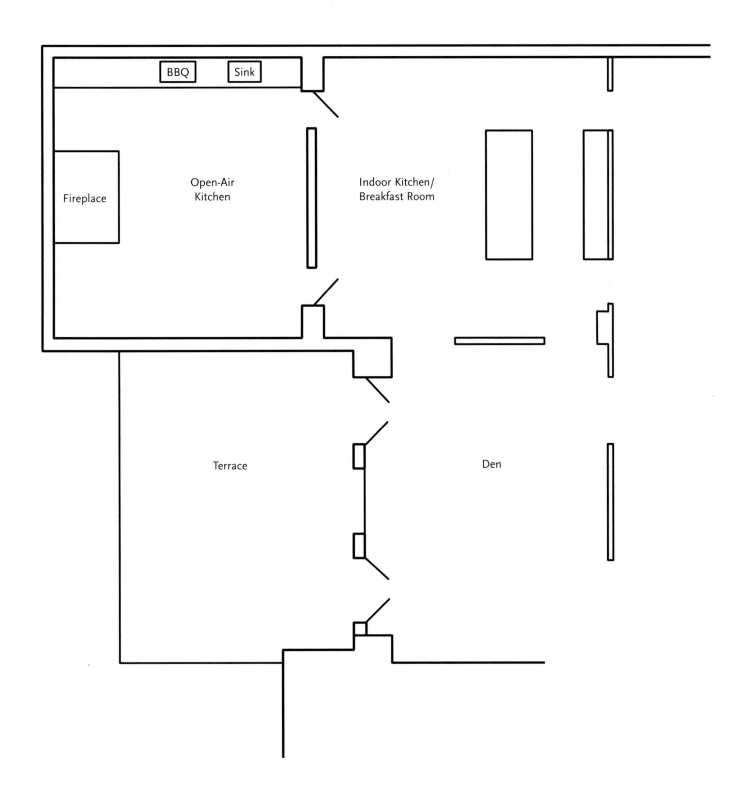

Fireplace

BBQ Sink

Open-Air Kitchen

Indoor Kitchen/ Breakfast Room

Terrace

Den

FACING: The kitchen side of the room is inset with a window equipped with operable louvers that can be opened to increase ventilation or closed to block views of a neighboring house. Molded brick pavers on the floor complement the walls and fireplace.

LEFT: The kitchen features a soapstone counter, stainless steel gas grill with side burner, sink and English pine cabinetry. Because the indoor kitchen is just steps away, the owners decided not to install a refrigerator, a money-saving move.

BELOW: Wood-clad steel braces support the vaulted ceiling and frame the treed setting. The design offers protection from the elements while keeping the owners connected to the yard.

Self-Contained Kitchen/Dining Center

DESIGN: Mark David Levine, Mark David Levine Design Group
PHOTOGRAPHS: Matilde Reyes

LOCATION: *Calabasas, California*
FEATURES: *two-sided grill/food prep center with wood pergola for sun protection*
KEY MATERIALS: *Spanish ceramic tile, Douglas fir, concrete, stucco*
SPECIAL TOUCHES: *refreshment center for storing condiments and cooling drinks*

By placing this well-equipped outdoor kitchen away from the house and positioning it to face the yard, landscape architect Mark David Levine made it possible for the person doing the cooking to interact with others and monitor activity on the lawn and in the pool—an important safety consideration for the owners, who have young children.

At half an acre, the yard didn't lack room but it was in need of better organization. Levine's landscape plan divided the lawn into four distinct zones—kitchen/dining area, main patio, pool and sitting area—all oriented toward the canyon views beyond the house. "The goal was to provide different use areas with lots of interesting textures and materials," he says. "We designed it both for beauty and functionality."

While some outdoor kitchens are placed next to the house, Levine wanted this kitchen to stand apart. The structure itself is a study in thoughtful design. Two islands, one with a combined grill/seating counter, the other with a prep counter and storage, face each other, forming a partially enclosed space with a concrete floor. A painted Douglas fir pergola helps shade the kitchen and the cook—important in a climate where summer temperatures can reach 100-plus degrees. Both the cooking and prep islands are concrete block covered in stucco and the counters are inlaid with Spanish ceramic tile. A refreshment center built into the prep island does everything from store condiments to cool drinks.

Levine paid special attention to the layout of the kitchen—for example, installing a long counter next to the grill so that setting down a platter of hot food could be accomplished in one swift move. "How you lay out the amenities of a kitchen is crucial to the success of the overall design—you don't want to have to walk three or four feet to set down a plate," he points out. "The goal is to find a way to combine efficiency and aesthetics."

SUN PROTECTION

If you live in an area of the country where summer temperatures soar, consider covering your kitchen with a trellis. And, if your climate permits, train vines to grow up and over the trellis, which will provide even more shade (an added bonus is that plants help to cool spaces through their natural process of transpiration). In a very hot climate, avoid a solid covering, as this will trap heat. Ceiling fans can also help circulate air through a covered kitchen.

The outdoor kitchen/dining center sits away from the house and faces the lawn, for easy monitoring of young children at play. The pergola will eventually be covered in vines for added sun protection.

FACING: Each piece of the Douglas fir pergola was individually sealed before construction, a technique that protects all sides of the wood from moisture and prevents rotting or bowing.

ABOVE LEFT: The concrete block grill island has been clad in stucco to match the house. A long counter next to the grill allows the cook to set down a plate of hot food in a single quick move. The counter is covered in Spanish ceramic tile and the patio is roughened concrete embedded with stone accents, a combination of materials that provides good traction. A side burner, warming drawers, under-counter refrigerator, and storage niches make cooking outdoors an efficient and pleasant endeavor.

BELOW LEFT: The bar-height dining counter facilitates communication between the cook and those waiting to eat.

FACING: The food prep/refreshment island provides extra work space and storage for utensils. It can also be used as a buffet counter during parties.

LEFT: The refreshment center includes a sink, an insulated bottle bath for keeping drinks cold, condiment bins, a cutting board that can slide out over the sink, a shelf rail for holding glasses, storage drawers, and a pullout trash container.

RESOURCES

ARCHITECTS AND DESIGNERS

CATHERINE CLEMENS
Clemens & Associates, Inc.
1012 Marquez Place, Suite 201
Santa Fe, NM 87501
(505) 982-4005
www.clemensandassociates.com

SCOTT COHEN
The Green Scene
6810 Canoga Avenue
Canoga Park, CA 91303
(818) 227-0740
www.greenscenelandscape.com

KEVIN CUNNINGHAM
Ultimate Outdoor Kitchens
Elburn, IL 60119
(888) GRILL-IT
www.uokdesigns.com

DALE DIBELLO AND ED EUBANKS
Eubanks Group Architects
790 S. Castell Avenue
New Braunfels, TX 78130
(830) 625-2652
www.eubanks-architects.com

MICHAEL DREEF AND ED EUBANKS
Eubanks Group Architects
3202 Argonne Street
Houston, TX 77098
(713) 522-2652
www.eubanks-architects.com

STEVEN EHRLICH
Steven Ehrlich Architects
10865 Washington Boulevard
Culver City, CA 90232
(310) 838-9700
www.s-ehrlich.com

COLLEEN HOLMES
New Leaf Landscape
5321 Derry Avenue, Suite D
Agoura Hills, CA 91301
(818) 597-4810

HUGH HUDDLESON
333 Bush Street, #3803
San Francisco, CA 94104
(415) 399-0711
www.hughhuddleson.com

MARK DAVID LEVINE
Mark David Levine Design Group
16861 Ventura Boulevard, Suite 200
Encino, CA 91436
(818) 793-6000
www.markdavidlevine.com

KATHERYN LOTT
2216 River Hills Road, Suite A
Austin, TX 78733
(512) 263-8778

CAMERON NAGEL
P.O. Box 10001
Portland, OR 97296
cameron@nwpalate.com

WILLIAM O'DOWD
511 Sapphire
Redondo Beach, CA 90277
(310) 316-0615

PETE PEDERSEN
Pedersen Associates Landscape Architecture
24 H Street
San Rafael, CA 94901
(415) 456-2070
www.pedersenassociates.com

BILL POSS
LYNDAL WILLIAMS
Poss Architecture, Planning & Interior Design
605 East Main Street
Aspen, CO 81611
(970) 925-4755
www.billposs.com

ROB ROBINSON
P.O. Box 759
Lincoln City, OR 97367
(541) 994-2865

TED TOKIO TANAKA
Ted Tokio Tanaka Architects
11307 Hindry Avenue
Los Angeles, CA 90045
(310) 484-1800
www.ttta.com

MICHELLE VAN DE VOORDE, ASLA
Elemental Design Group
1200 Blue Ridge Drive
Boulder Creek, CA 95006
(831) 338-1709
www.elementaldesign.com